FIREPIT FEAST

FIREPIT FEAST

Adventurous Recipes for Live-Fire Cooking

Diana Yen

Photographs by Diana Yen and Dylan Gordon

ARTISAN | NEW YORK

Library of Congress Cataloging-in-Publication Data

Names: Yen, Diana, author, photographer. | Gordon, Dylan, photographer.
Title: Firepit feast : adventurous recipes for live-fire cooking / Diana Yen ; photographs by Diana Yen and Dylan Gordon.
Description: New York : Artisan, [2025] | Includes index.
Identifiers: LCCN 2024050119 | ISBN 9781648293672 (hardback)
Subjects: LCSH: Fireplace cooking. | LCGFT: Cookbooks.
Classification: LCC TX840.F5 Y46 2025 | DDC 641.5/78—dc23 /eng/20241205
LC record available at https://lccn.loc.gov/2024050119

Design by Suet Chong

Artisan books may be purchased in bulk for business, educational, or promotional use. For information, please contact your local bookseller or the Hachette Book Group Special Markets Department at special.markets@hbgusa.com.

The publisher is not responsible for websites (or their content) that are not owned by the publisher.

The Hachette Speakers Bureau provides a wide range of authors for speaking events. To find out more, go to hachettespeakersbureau.com or email HachetteSpeakers@hbgusa.com.

Published by Artisan,
an imprint of Workman Publishing,
a division of Hachette Book Group, Inc.
1290 Avenue of the Americas
New York, NY 10104
artisanbooks.com

The Artisan name and logo are registered trademarks of Hachette Book Group, Inc.

Printed in China (APO) on responsibly sourced paper

First printing, March 2025

10 9 8 7 6 5 4 3 2 1

For my mother,

Annie,

who passed down her joy of cooking to me

CONTENTS

INTRODUCTION

There's nothing quite like the flavor of food that comes from live-fire cooking: whether it's juicy, charred chicken skewers or meltingly tender sweet potatoes thrown over coals to roast slowly, everything eaten fireside seems to taste more delicious.

So many people have a firepit in their backyard these days, and there's a whole world of possibilities to cook with it beyond toasting marshmallows. Firepits are fantastic for cooking because they give dishes that extra depth of flavor and transform simple gatherings into culinary adventures for everyone to enjoy.

Cooking over fire is primal and intuitive, yet many of us feel intimidated taming flames to create a meal. Here you'll learn that there's no need to be a pitmaster or even an outdoorsy type to confidently cook over a firepit. Filled with approachable recipe ideas and vivid imagery, this book is designed to spark inspiration whether you're planning a cozy meal with family and friends in your backyard or ready to up the food on your next camping trip.

The recipes are organized by cooking equipment, because so much of our approach to cooking outdoors depends on what you have available. You can start out simply by tossing a few skewers on the grill or take your cast-iron skillet from the stovetop to the great outdoors. Once you become firepit obsessed, you might decide that you need a bigger Dutch oven to feed a group of hungry diners. These delicious recipes will get you going no matter where you're starting out (think peel 'n' eat shrimp scampi foil packets, ultra-gooey Cuban pudgy pies, veggie-loving dishes for everyone), and they include tips to keep things fun, not stressful.

Fire cooking is all about trusting your instincts and engaging your senses. You'll quickly discover that you can cook the foods that you crave and meals that nourish you, instead of settling for plain old hot dogs, while enjoying the outdoors. Most importantly, cooking over fire will make you feel empowered.

There are countless ways to build a fire and cook with it, but here's one golden rule I swear by: the slow burn. Let the flames die down until the heat is even and steady. Once you hit that sweet spot, your fire is ready for cooking. Whether grilling over the coals or burying your foods *in* the coals, this hands-on experience will bring out your inner chef. Tending to your food while the scents of sizzling meats and roasting vegetables fill the air makes you more invested in the result. Firepit cooking offers a soulful recharge and rewards you with unforgettable meals shared with loved ones around the fire's flickering warmth.

EQUIPMENT: ESSENTIALS YOU NEED TO START COOKING

Cooking over a fire is pretty low-key when it comes to gear—all you really need to begin is a firepit with a grill grate. Raid your kitchen for tools that might come in handy. For example, the same cast-iron pan you use indoors can be used over the firepit, and the same skewers you employ on your gas grill can be repurposed as well. Once you start diving deeper into the world of fire cooking (and trust me, it's easy to get hooked), you'll realize there's a whole universe of equipment and tools out there waiting to be explored.

The Basics

Whether you're a seasoned outdoor grill master or cooking over flames for the first time, let's talk about the essential equipment you'll need to kick-start your fire-cooking adventure.

Firepit with grill grate: This is the heart of your outdoor cooking setup. A firepit outfitted with a grill grate provides the foundation for your culinary exploration as well as a cozy place to gather with others. An adjustable grill grate is ideal so you can quickly lift and lower it to adjust the cooking temperature. Firepits come in a range, from the basic pit-and-grate combinations and smokeless pits for the backyard (see Resources, page 232) to the built-in ones at campgrounds.

Long-handled tongs: Tongs are your trusty sidekick for maneuvering food over the flames without getting too close yourself. They're essential for flipping veggies, rotating skewers, and moving hot coals around.

Firepit poker: A fire poker is a long-handled tool designed to help you tend to your flames with ease. Whether you're prodding the logs into the perfect arrangement or stirring up those hot embers, it's your go-to tool for keeping the fire roaring. Many of them even have a little built-in hook that's ideal for lifting the lid of a Dutch oven without having to remove the coals.

Heat-resistant gloves: Keep your hands safe from high heat with a sturdy pair of heat-resistant gloves. Whether you're adjusting logs or handling hot cookware, these gloves will protect your hands from burns.

Charcoal chimney starter: Say goodbye to lighter fluid and hello to chimney starters. This is a straightforward device, basically a metal tube with a grate that makes lighting charcoal a breeze. Simply fill the chimney with charcoal, place it over your firepit, and ignite fire starters or paper in the bottom. In no time, you'll have hot coals ready for cooking.

Cast-iron skillet: A pan you may already have in your kitchen, the cast-iron skillet is equally useful over the firepit. Use it to sear pork chops, fry eggs, or even bake desserts. Its heavy-duty quality and heat retention make it an essential for outdoor cooking. I like using the 10-inch (25 cm) size for cooking small bites and appetizers, but I rely on my 12-inch (30 cm) when I'm cooking larger meals or serving multiple guests.

Cast-iron camp Dutch oven: You might be eyeing the Le Creuset on your stovetop, wondering if it'll do. Well, yes and no. Camping Dutch ovens (see Resources, page 232) are made entirely from cast iron, have support legs for sitting over coals, and have a flat, flanged lid that holds coals (especially handy when you're baking over the flames). These pans even have a bail handle to hang on a tripod for cooking over the fire. If I'm making something like a stew or soup and only need a lower heat source, I'll grab my enameled Dutch oven to use in a pinch.

Pie iron: Perhaps the most underrated cooking tool, the pie iron is essentially two metal cast-iron pans that are hinged together like a clamshell, creating a little cooking chamber. You can use a pie iron to make all sorts of goodies, from

CAST IRON CARE

Cast iron is the go-to cookware for firepit cooking, and taking care of it is the key to keeping it in top shape. After using your cast-iron skillet, let it cool down a bit before cleaning. Rinse it with warm water and use a brush, sponge, or chain-mail scrubber to remove any food debris. If you can, try to skip the dish soap, as it can affect the seasoning of the pan. Dry the skillet with a dish towel, then place it over low heat until all the moisture is gone. Finally, give it a quick rub with a little vegetable oil to keep it in great condition and prevent rust.

perfectly crispy grilled cheese sandwiches to delicious hand pies, all cooked up in minutes. The iron has this awesome vintage vibe that everyone loves, and it's a surefire way to get your friends excited about cooking together outdoors. Plus, it's super easy to use, making it a must-have for any camping adventure or backyard bonfire.

Instant-read thermometer: Take the guesswork out of grilling with an instant-read thermometer. Whether you're cooking steaks, chicken, or fish, a thermometer ensures your food reaches the perfect internal temperature for safety and flavor.

Cooking utensils: Fireproof cooking utensils come in handy for outdoor cooking adventures. Keep an eye out for ones with long handles made from heat-resistant materials—perfect for maneuvering food over the fire. One of my favorite tools is the trusty fish spatula. Its slim, flexible design makes it a total multitasker, whether you're delicately flipping seafood, frying up eggs, or mastering the perfect pancake.

Headlamp: When the sun starts to set and darkness creeps in, it can get pretty tricky to see what you're cooking. That's where the headlamp comes in handy. It's your beacon of light, a hands-free tool to navigate through the darkness and ensure you can see the delicious food you're making.

Grill brush: After a cookout, you might notice some food residue on your grill grate. To keep it in great shape, simply wait until it cools down, then give it a quick scrub with a grill brush.

USING THIS BOOK

Now that you've got your gear all set up, let's chat about how to make the most of this book. While I've included some really helpful tips and tricks for you to use while you're cooking, I also know that once the fire gets going, something instinctual takes over. Your brain just goes, "FIRE, I made a FIRE!" And you might just wanna stare into those hypnotic flames and forget all about what you were supposed to be doing.

That's why it's important to remember these key things:

Read the Recipe

Before you cook, read the recipe—and I mean all the way through. It'll help you grasp the general flow of your cooking, what you can prep ahead, what needs your immediate attention, and when you can kick back a bit and let things simmer. You don't want to miss that crucial step where you were supposed to marinate your meat an hour in advance. When you're cooking outdoors, small oversights can end up costing you time later on (e.g., dashing back into the house to wash salad greens).

Start Early

Cooking outdoors is different in a major way—it's not the same as walking into your kitchen and turning a knob to heat the pan. Remember, you are building a fire from scratch, and things can be unpredictable, whether it's the weather or, *oops*, forgetting the kindling. So, as a general rule, plan to start the fire at least an hour before you plan to cook. I typically like to do it before it gets dark and visibility becomes an issue. You might start the fire in the late afternoon, for example, if you're having an evening meal.

Prep It Out

Sheet pans are lifesavers for outdoor cooking. Simply gather all your prepped ingredients and line them up on a sheet pan, which is perfect for holding chopped veggies, skewers, ramekins with oil and sauces, and seasonings like salt and pepper. Then, when the fire gets going, you won't have to scramble around searching for the components of your meal.

Using Your Senses

As much as I'd love to give you precise cooking times and consistent results for each recipe, nothing is guaranteed with a live fire—it's always changing. So it's up to you to rely on your senses to determine when your food is ready. If you toss ingredients into a skillet and don't hear that satisfying sizzle, it's time to amp up the heat by rotating a log or piling the coals higher. And if a skewer seems to be cooking too quickly, trust your gut—it probably is! Try slowing things down by adjusting the grill grate or spreading out the coals. Cooking over a fire is all about gaining experience over time, and it's okay to make a few mistakes along the way.

Always Keep an Eye on the Fire

You've finally got your fire going and prepped your ingredients, and you're ready to cook. But wait . . . you forgot to slice the scallions, and now you're tempted to run inside to finish up. DON'T DO IT unless you have another pair of eyes on that fire. Once your fire has started, it's your responsibility to maintain it for the safety of everyone around you. Ask someone else to grab a forgotten item in the kitchen or to take over watching the fire before you look away.

Put It Out

And finally, it's the end of the night and bellies are full. The last thing to do is to extinguish the fire before saying good night. Start by spreading out the embers and logs using a poker or shovel. Then slowly pour water over the embers, ensuring they are completely soaked. Stir the embers and remaining ashes to make sure all hot spots are cooled. Even if you see only a couple of glowing coals, err on the side of safety and repeat the process until there are no more glowing embers and everything feels cool to the touch. Finally, dispose of the ashes the next day, once they are completely cold.

HOW TO BUILD A COOKING FIRE

There's a real beauty in building a fire—it's like a little test of patience and respect rolled into one. Sometimes it doesn't cooperate right away; you might wrestle with that initial spark. And even when you've got it roaring just how you like it, it's a constant dance of keeping the fire going.

But you know what? That's the magic of working with fire. I've come to learn that it's not just about the flames; it's about staying in the moment and listening to your intuition. Let fire be your guide, my friend. Once you've got your fire going, the fun is just beginning. Let's dive into how to harness your cooking temperatures to optimize cooking over the fire.

Fire Cooking Zones

Think of cooking zones as designated areas within your firepit where you can control the heat to cook different types of food. For example, if you're searing pork chops over high heat and simmering a stew over gentle embers, having cooking zones ensures that each dish gets the right amount of heat.

It's ideal to create three cooking zones: the burning zone, where logs are added to create new coals (too hot for cooking); the cooking zone, with glowing coals and direct heat for searing or grilling; and the indirect heat zone, with fewer to no coals for low-temperature cooking and for keeping foods warm. Ultimately, your goal is to have enough space to control the heat and cook delicious food. (For more on cooking zones, see page 19.)

STEPS TO BUILD A FIRE

1. **Prepare your firepit:** Start by clearing your firepit of any debris or ashes from previous fires. Make sure it's on stable ground and at least 5 feet (1.5 m) away from shrubs, tall grass, or dry leaves and 10 feet (3 m) away from building structures. Steer clear of overhanging trees.

2. **Gather your gear:** Grab your firewood, kindling, and any fire-starting essentials like paper or fire starters. And don't forget the heat-resistant gloves.

3. **Work log cabin–style:** Arrange a base of two larger firewood pieces in your firepit, laying them parallel about 1 foot (0.3 m) apart. The space in between is where you'll add your tinder. You can use fire starters, paper, or dry leaves. Next, lay twigs, sticks, or other fast-combusting wood pieces over the tinder, starting with smaller pieces and building up to larger ones. Then top it off with two more pieces of wood, perpendicular to the logs below them (remember those

Lincoln Logs you played with as a kid?). Between the second layer of logs, add one or two small pieces of wood that will catch easily. Continue stacking logs to the desired height.

4. **Light it up:** Use matches or a long lighter to ignite the tinder. Watch as your fire begins to catch and come to life. Have some extra smaller pieces of wood on the side in case you need to add more to get it going.

5. **Feed the fire:** Once your fire is burning steadily, add more firewood gradually. Keep in mind that larger logs will burn more slowly and produce more heat

over a longer period, while smaller logs will burn faster and produce intense heat quickly. Hardwoods like oak and maple burn hotter and longer than softwoods like pine.

6. **Create your zones:** Some dishes, like s'mores and pudgy pies, can be cooked over flames as soon as they get started. For most other kinds of cooking, you'll need to wait for your fire to burn down to glowing embers for steady, even heat. This will take at least 30 minutes and up to 1 hour. Next, you'll want to create three zones for maximum cooking control.

THE THREE ZONES

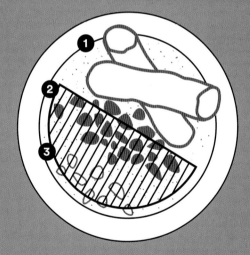

BURNING ZONE (1): Push the burning logs to one side of the firepit. This will be the zone where you can continue to feed the fire with logs as needed to sustain the heat. For longer cooking times, continue to rake fresh coals from your burning zone into your cooking zone to maintain a steady heat.

COOKING ZONE (2): Gather the hot, glowing coals into the center to create your cooking zone. Make sure they are under the area where your grill grate will go. This is where most of your cooking happens; think grilling and skillet dishes.

INDIRECT HEAT ZONE (3): Leave some space on one end where you'll be cooking with fewer to no coals, depending on your needs. This will be a spot to simmer Dutch oven dishes or to keep food warm.

What do you do if you find yourself tight on space with a small firepit? Focus on building a two-zone fire, where you have a cooking zone, and then a small burning zone to the side where you can add logs to sustain the fire.

7. **Adjust the heat:** Depending on what you're cooking, you may need to adjust the position of the wood to control the heat. To increase heat, add larger logs or stack logs closer together to restrict airflow, causing the fire to burn hotter and slower. To reduce heat, add smaller logs or spread out the logs to allow more airflow, which will encourage the fire to burn faster and cooler. While you're cooking, you can pile up the coals for more heat or spread them out for less. It's all about finding that perfect balance. If you have an adjustable grill grate, raising and lowering it is also an option.

8. **Stay safe:** Remember to always keep an eye on your fire and never leave it unattended. For safety, keep a pail of water or fire extinguisher nearby. When you're done cooking, make sure to fully extinguish the fire with water or sand.

How to Test the Heat Level

Because of the ever-changing nature of a fire, you can't just set wood to an exact temperature. So how can you gauge how hot a fire is? Well, you gotta feel it (safely, of course). When I first heard of the "hand test," I thought, "No way am I putting my hands over the fire," but it's actually not that scary. It's kinda like when you open an oven and feel the heat to see if it's good to go.

Simply extend your hand about 5 inches (13 cm) above your cooking surface and begin counting.

SIZZLE METHOD

Okay, there's another way to test heat that feels a little less caveman. It's ideal for when you're cooking in a skillet or Dutch oven. To check if the pan has reached a medium-high heat, just flick a few drops of water onto the surface with your fingers. When it's ready, the drops will bounce and sizzle in a second or so, which means you're all set to start cooking.

For high heat: If you can't hold your hand there for more than 1 to 2 seconds, you've got some serious sizzle going on. This zone is ideal for searing meats or giving veggies a quick char.

For medium-high heat: The sweet spot usually lands somewhere between high and medium, at 2 to 4 seconds. Medium-high is the kind of heat where you can sauté food without burning it and keep things cooking at a moderate pace.

For medium heat: If you can hold your hand there for 4 to 5 seconds, you're in a zone that is ideal for foods that have a slightly longer cooking time.

For low heat: If you can hold your hand there for more than 5 seconds, it's like a mellow warmth from the flames. This zone is great for slow-cooking meats and toasting marshmallows without burning them.

Remember, safety first! Always use caution around open flames, and if the fire feels too hot, trust your instincts and give yourself and your firepit a little breathing room.

Types of Wood

Wood will be your go-to essential for fire cooking, no doubt about it. But here's the thing: even if you're a top-notch cook, starting with damp wood is going to lead to frustration and a lot of smoke. Trust me, I've been there. My tip? Opt for seasoned hardwoods—they'll get your fire going more quickly and make your cooking sesh way more enjoyable. Seasoned hardwood is wood that has been dried out for at least six months, which means it burns hotter and cleaner with less smoke.

When it comes to sourcing your wood, start local. Check out nearby farms or ranches; they often sell wood by the pallet, which will save you some dough while giving back to your community. And check out hardware and grocery stores—they usually have some great wood selections, too.

WOOD TYPES

When it comes to cooking over a fire, choosing the right type of firewood can make all the difference. Each type of wood imparts its own unique flavor to your food and is best suited for specific cooking techniques.

Type of Wood	Flavor	Uses
Apple	Sweet and fruity	Adds a subtle sweetness to everything, especially poultry, pork, and lamb
Cherry	Mild and fruity	Enhances the flavor of meats, seafood, and vegetables
Maple	Sweet and mild	Fantastic choice for pork, poultry, and veggies
Pecan	Light and nutty	Perfect for barbecue dishes, like ribs, chicken, and brisket
Oak	Robust and versatile	Pairs well with a variety of foods, from beef to fish
Hickory	Robust and smoky	Adds a rich, smoky flavor to meats; a classic choice for barbecue lovers
Mesquite	Bold and intense	Ideal for grilling steaks, lamb, and other hearty meats

Firewood Coals, Lump Charcoal, and Briquettes

When you're craving that cozy crackling wood-fire vibe for a laid-back hangout and cookout, go ahead and build a wood fire. Once your fire begins to burn down, the hot, glowing coals left behind burn hotter and cleaner than wood, making them ideal for outdoor cooking. Plus, these firewood coals add that signature smoky flavor to your food.

But hey, we all have those moments when the sun's going down and we need dinner on the table ASAP, right? That's where lump charcoal and briquettes come to the rescue. If you're short on time, they're your convenient solution to get cooking right away.

Here's a quick rundown on each:

Lump charcoal: Think of this as the natural speedy option. Made from hardwood, it's the next best thing to cooking over a wood fire. It burns hot and lights fast, perfect for quick grilling sessions. Just be aware that some of the pieces can be huge; because it's natural, it doesn't have standard sizing. And feel free to combine lump charcoal with your wood charcoal in your firepit to speed up the cooking process.

Briquettes: These are the reliable, affordable, steady performers, made from charcoal dust and binders, ensuring consistent heat for longer cooking times. Because they are smaller and uniform in size, they are easier to use to maintain even, steady heat. I like using these specifically for firepit baking with a Dutch oven.

How to Light a Chimney for Coals

First, place the chimney in the middle of your firepit. Then, fill it up with charcoal—lump or briquettes, your choice. Now, toss some crumpled newspaper or a couple of fire starters in the chamber underneath. Light the paper or fire starters and let the flames do their thing. As the coals heat up, you'll notice them turning gray and developing a covering of ash. Once they're ready (usually in 15 to 20 minutes), carefully pour them out into your firepit. Just remember to handle the chimney with care, and you'll be cooking in no time.

For dishes that take longer than an hour to cook, you may need to replenish with another batch of hot coals. Repeat using the same process as before, and if you find yourself running out of room in your pit to light your chimney, try placing it on the grate of another grill or on fire-safe bricks placed on your patio.

G

When it comes to firepit cooking, grilling is usually the first thing that comes to mind. Grilling over an open flame isn't just about charred burgers and hot dogs (although, don't get me wrong, those have their time and place). It's about embracing the versatility of the grill and understanding that, despite being one of the simplest ways to cook, it also requires your attention and patience.

Cooking on the grill lets you pick and choose and build a menu pretty easily, so you can have a few things going at once. Here you'll find recipes that celebrate the smoky, charred quality that only a grill can deliver. From vibrant grilled veggies to vegetarian Grilled Halloumi and Artichoke Burgers to an impressive Smoky Spatchcocked Chicken with Herby Yogurt Drizzle, each dish is meant to showcase the unique flavors that come from cooking over an open flame.

Here are some extra tips to get you started. If you don't have a grill rack and are planning to purchase one, opt for an adjustable model with a large cooking area. This way, you can easily lower and raise it to react to changing temperatures and have more space to spread out while cooking. Another tip: *Always be oiling*. It's easy to forget to oil your grates before placing food on them, so keep a ramekin of neutral oil and a heatproof brush on standby—this will ensure none of your food sticks to the grates when flipping it. So get that fire going, grab your tongs, and get ready to dive into a world of bold flavors.

GRILLED STONE FRUIT, TOMATOES & SNAP PEAS WITH BURRATA

SERVES 4

Neutral oil (such as canola or avocado oil), for brushing

2 tablespoons extra-virgin olive oil, plus more for drizzling

2 tablespoons red wine vinegar

2 teaspoons honey

Pinch of red pepper flakes

Kosher salt and freshly ground black pepper

3 medium, firm heirloom tomatoes (about 1 pound/ 455 g), stemmed, sliced in half horizontally

2 pounds (910 g) mixed firm stone fruit (such as peaches, nectarines, plums, or apricots), halved, or quartered if large

8 ounces (225 g) sugar snap peas, trimmed, strings removed

One 8-ounce (225 g) ball burrata cheese, at room temperature

2 tablespoons freshly torn basil leaves

2 tablespoons chopped fresh dill

Flaky sea salt

Unlike the usual anticipation for summer fruit to fully ripen, in this case, opting for firm fruit is ideal as the fruit turns caramelized and juicy on the grill. Any combination of peaches, nectarines, plums, or apricots would be ideal. Overripe fruits, on the other hand, tend to become mushy. To enhance the flavors, the fruit is marinated in a tangy vinaigrette before grilling. Make sure to reserve some of the delicious marinade to drizzle over the salad at the end.

Prepare a fire for medium-high heat (see page 20), set a grate over it, and brush the grate with neutral oil.

In a large bowl, whisk together the olive oil, vinegar, honey, and red pepper flakes. Season the marinade with kosher salt and black pepper to taste. Add the tomatoes and stone fruit cut side down to absorb the marinade, and gently toss to coat. Let marinate for 10 minutes, tossing occasionally. Using a slotted spoon, transfer the tomatoes and stone fruit to a sheet pan. Reserve the marinade; it should be full of delicious juices from the fruit and will be used to finish the dish. Add the snap peas to the sheet pan. Drizzle the peas with olive oil and toss to coat. Season all over with kosher salt and black pepper.

Grill the tomatoes and stone fruit cut side down, along with the snap peas, leaving undisturbed until char marks appear, 2 to 3 minutes; then flip over and cook until softened, 1 to 2 more minutes. Transfer to a serving platter.

Tear the ball of burrata into large pieces to top the salad. Drizzle with the reserved marinade and top with the basil and dill. Season with flaky salt and black pepper.

CHUNKY ZUCCHINI TOASTS WITH WHIPPED HERBY FETA

SERVES 4

Neutral oil (such as canola or avocado oil), for brushing

5 to 6 small or 3 medium zucchini, ends trimmed, sliced in half lengthwise and scored inside

¼ cup (60 ml) extra-virgin olive oil

Kosher salt and freshly ground black pepper

4 thick slices crusty sourdough bread, cut into halves

Juice of ½ lemon

½ cup (125 g) Whipped Herby Feta (page 221)

Hot honey, for drizzling (see Note)

Flaky sea salt

2 tablespoons chopped tender herbs (such as dill, basil, or mint)

Chunks of perfectly charred zucchini, generously spooned over grilled toasts slathered with a creamy herbed feta spread, might just be one of the best combinations of all time. Cutting the zucchini into halves and scoring the insides makes them easier to flip on the grill and helps maintain their texture. For the best flavor, opt for small zucchini that make their debut in early summer.

Prepare a fire for medium-high heat (see page 20), set a grate over it, and brush the grate with neutral oil.

If using larger zucchini, scrape the seeds from the middle with a spoon and discard. On a sheet pan, brush the zucchini halves with some of the olive oil and season with kosher salt and pepper. Brush the bread on both sides with the remaining olive oil and season with kosher salt and pepper.

Place the zucchini cut side down onto the grill grate and cook until tender and charred, 3 to 5 minutes on each side. Grill the bread slices until char marks appear, 1 to 2 minutes on each side. Set aside to cool. Transfer the zucchini to a sheet pan and drizzle the lemon juice all over. Let cool slightly, then cut into bite-size pieces, discarding any tough ends.

Spread the toasts with the whipped feta and top with zucchini chunks. Drizzle with hot honey. Finish with flaky salt and sprinkle with the fresh herbs.

NOTE: *If you don't have hot honey, try mixing regular honey with a few dashes of hot sauce for a spicy kick.*

TAHINI CAESAR SALAD WITH CRAGGY ZA'ATAR CROUTONS

SERVES 4

½ cup (50 g) grated Parmesan

¼ cup (60 ml) extra-virgin olive oil

¼ cup (60 g) tahini, stirred smooth

¼ cup (60 ml) water

2 tablespoons fresh lemon juice

1 tablespoon plain yogurt

1 garlic clove, finely grated

Kosher salt and freshly ground black pepper

Neutral oil (such as canola or avocado oil), for brushing

1 thick slice country bread

2 heads romaine lettuce, washed and dried, cut lengthwise into halves

1 teaspoon za'atar spice

Here's a twist on the classic Caesar salad with a smoky touch. Romaine holds up well on the grill, coming out caramelized and charred on the edges. A creamy tahini dressing is easy to make—no eggs or anchovies needed. Finish off your salad with crunchy za'atar-spiced croutons.

In a small bowl, whisk together ¼ cup (25 g) of the Parmesan, 2 tablespoons of the olive oil, the tahini, water, lemon juice, yogurt, and garlic. Continue mixing until smooth. Season with a big pinch of salt and pepper to taste.

Prepare a fire for medium-high heat (see page 20), set a grate over it, and brush the grate with neutral oil.

Place the bread and romaine halves on a sheet pan. Put 1 tablespoon of the olive oil, a pinch of salt, and the za'atar spice in a small bowl and stir to combine. Brush the bread on both sides with the za'atar mixture. Brush the romaine halves with the remaining 1 tablespoon olive oil and season with salt.

Grill the romaine for 3 minutes, cut side down, pressing with your tongs to give it a nice char. Flip over and grill for another 2 minutes. Grill the bread until golden brown and crisp on the outside, 1 to 2 minutes on each side. Set aside to cool. Transfer the romaine to a cutting board. Let cool slightly, then chop into 2-inch (5 cm) pieces, discarding the tough ends. Place in a salad bowl.

Tear the bread into craggy croutons. Using your hands, toss the romaine with just enough tahini dressing to coat, then top it with the remaining ¼ cup (25 g) Parmesan and the croutons. Any leftover dressing can be stored in an airtight container in the refrigerator for up to 3 days.

PATATAS BRAVAS POTATO SALAD

SERVES 4 TO 6

2 pounds (910 g) baby Yukon Gold potatoes

1 tablespoon kosher salt, plus more to taste

⅓ cup (80 g) mayonnaise

2 teaspoons sherry vinegar

3 garlic cloves, finely grated

1 teaspoon tomato paste

1 teaspoon smoked paprika

¾ teaspoon ground chipotle

3 tablespoons extra-virgin olive oil, plus more for drizzling

Neutral oil (such as canola or avocado oil), for brushing

½ small red onion, thinly sliced

2 tablespoons chopped parsley leaves

For a vibrant take on traditional potato salad, try this version inspired by the Spanish tapa. It features crispy potatoes with smoky spices and a drizzle of spicy mayo. It's a fantastic side for your next barbecue.

Place the potatoes in a large pot and cover with 2 inches (5 cm) of water. Season generously with salt and bring to a boil over high heat. Reduce the heat to medium and continue to simmer until the potatoes are fork-tender, 10 to 12 minutes. Drain through a large strainer and set aside to cool slightly.

Meanwhile, make the spicy mayo sauce. In a bowl, stir together the mayonnaise, vinegar, half of the garlic, the tomato paste, ½ teaspoon of the paprika, ¼ teaspoon of the ground chipotle, and a pinch of salt.

In a small bowl, make the spice mix. Combine the tablespoon of salt, the remaining ½ teaspoon paprika, and the remaining ½ teaspoon ground chipotle.

Once the potatoes are cool enough to handle, cut into halves lengthwise and transfer back to the pot. Drizzle the potatoes all over with the olive oil and add the remaining garlic. Place the lid on the pot, lift, and with both hands give the pot a few strong shakes. Leave the pot covered and set it aside until you're ready to grill.

Prepare a fire for medium-high heat (see page 20), set a grate over it, and brush the grate with neutral oil.

Transfer the potatoes to a sheet pan. Place the potatoes on the grill grate and cook until golden brown and crispy on both sides, turning halfway, 12 to 15 minutes total. Transfer the potatoes to a serving bowl with the red onions. Drizzle with olive oil and toss with the spice mix to combine. Finish with a drizzle of the spicy mayo sauce and a sprinkle of parsley. Serve warm.

SPICY MAYO

CUMIN GRILLED CARROTS WITH LEMONY YOGURT

SERVES 4

Neutral oil (such as canola or avocado oil), for brushing

2 bunches (about 1½ pounds/ 680 g) carrots, scrubbed, tops trimmed to 1 inch (2.5 cm), and halved lengthwise (or quartered if large)

2 tablespoons extra-virgin olive oil

2 teaspoons ground cumin

Kosher salt and freshly ground black pepper

1 cup (240 g) Lemony Yogurt Sauce (page 221)

2 teaspoons chili crisp

2 tablespoons chopped toasted pistachios

1 tablespoon torn mint leaves

What takes a platter of grilled vegetables from meh to freakin' delicious? The secret is all in the sauce. These cumin-spiced carrots are grilled to enhance their sweetness and develop a caramelized crust, then served over a tangy lemon yogurt sauce, complemented by a drizzle of chili crisp for a touch of heat. Feel free to swap out the yogurt sauce and experiment with different spin-offs: Whipped Herby Feta (page 221) and Walnut Romesco Sauce (page 40) would both work wonderfully.

Prepare a fire for medium heat (see page 20), set a grate over it, and brush the grate with neutral oil. Make sure to adjust your heat so it isn't too high; carrots have a high sugar content that can cause them to burn quickly.

Place the carrots on a large sheet pan. Toss with the olive oil and cumin. Season with salt and pepper. Grill the carrots until charred and crisp-tender, turning occasionally, 15 to 20 minutes total. Smaller carrots tend to cook faster; move the finished carrots to the cooler part of the grill while the others continue to cook.

Spread the yogurt sauce onto a serving platter. Arrange the carrots on top. Drizzle with the chili crisp and scatter the pistachios and mint leaves to finish.

SPICED CAULIFLOWER STEAKS WITH WALNUT ROMESCO SAUCE

SERVES 4

Neutral oil (such as canola or avocado oil), for brushing

½ cup (120 ml) extra-virgin olive oil

1 tablespoon red wine vinegar

2 garlic cloves, finely grated

1 teaspoon honey

½ teaspoon smoked paprika

½ teaspoon ground cumin

¼ teaspoon red pepper flakes

Kosher salt

2 small heads cauliflower (about 4 pounds/1.8 kg), outer leaves removed and stems trimmed

Freshly ground black pepper

¾ cup (170 g) Walnut Romesco Sauce (recipe follows)

½ cup (75 g) crumbled feta cheese

¼ cup (15 g) chopped parsley leaves

Slicing cauliflower into slabs ensures maximum grill contact, allowing it to become tender and caramelized all over. And if one of your guests is vegetarian, these cauliflower "steaks" perform double duty as a vegetarian main or hearty side. Serve them over a generous pool of sweet and smoky Walnut Romesco Sauce and finish it off with salty crumbles of feta.

Prepare a fire for medium heat (see page 20), set a grate over it, and brush the grate with neutral oil.

In a small bowl, combine the olive oil, vinegar, garlic, honey, paprika, cumin, and red pepper flakes. Season with salt to taste.

Standing the cauliflower up on its stem, slice vertically into ½-inch-thick (1.3 cm) slices. Keeping the stem helps the cauliflower florets stay intact. You'll end up with a few large steaks and big chunks (make sure to use pieces that fit on the grill grates). Transfer the cauliflower to a sheet pan and brush with the spiced olive oil mixture. Season with salt and black pepper. Grill the cauliflower until deeply charred and crisp-tender, turning halfway, 10 to 12 minutes total.

Spread the romesco sauce on a serving platter. Arrange the cauliflower steaks on top. Finish with the crumbled feta and parsley.

Walnut Romesco Sauce

**MAKES ABOUT 1½ CUPS
(340 G)**

One 16-ounce (454 g) jar
roasted red peppers, drained

⅓ cup (40 g) toasted walnuts,
roughly chopped

1 garlic clove, smashed and
peeled

1 teaspoon smoked paprika

½ teaspoon red pepper
flakes, plus more to taste

⅓ cup (80 ml) extra-virgin
olive oil

1 tablespoon sherry vinegar
or red wine vinegar

Kosher salt

A nutty and smoky sauce inspired by the Catalan classic,
this quick and simple version leans on jarred red peppers to
cut down on prep time. Blitz them in the food processor with
walnuts, and you'll end up with a vivid red sauce that goes
along well with grilled meats, fish, and charred veggies.

Chop the red peppers into big chunks. In a food processor
or blender, pulse together the red peppers, walnuts, garlic,
paprika, and red pepper flakes, scraping down the sides of
the bowl as needed. With the machine still running, add the
olive oil and vinegar in a slow stream. Blend until the sauce
reaches a pureed but slightly chunky consistency. Season
with salt to taste and add more red pepper flakes if desired.
Serve immediately, or store in an airtight container in the
refrigerator for up to 1 week.

SMOKY GRILLED CORN

SERVES 4

Neutral oil (such as canola or avocado oil), for brushing

4 ears of corn, silks removed, husks peeled back

Corn on the cob is made for the grill: the char brings out its natural sweetness, while cooking it over a fire adds smoky depths. Whether you're a fan of simply grilled corn or want to try a classic creamy Mexican street corn, corn with Asian umami flavors from miso butter and a sprinkle of furikake, or a Greek-inspired twist with Whipped Herby Feta—there's something here for everyone. Choose-your-own-adventure is my favorite approach for a party; double the amount of corn and provide all three toppings for guests to dress up their own.

Prepare a fire for medium-high heat (see page 20), set a grate over it, and brush the grate with neutral oil.

Grill the corn, turning occasionally, until the kernels are charred in spots and tender, 10 to 12 minutes. Transfer to a platter. Serve as is or with desired toppings.

VARIATIONS

Mexican Grilled Corn

¼ cup (60 g) Mexican crema or sour cream

¼ cup (60 g) mayonnaise

¼ cup (10 g) chopped cilantro leaves

½ teaspoon ancho or chipotle chile powder, plus more for sprinkling

1 garlic clove, finely grated

Kosher salt

¼ cup (55 g) crumbled Cotija cheese

Lime wedges, for serving

While the corn is grilling, in a bowl, stir together the crema, mayonnaise, 2 tablespoons of the cilantro, the chile powder, and the garlic. Taste the sauce and season with salt if needed. Using a brush or spoon, slather the sauce onto the cooked corn to coat. Sprinkle the corn with more chile powder, then top with the Cotija and remaining 2 tablespoons cilantro. Serve with lime wedges for squeezing over.

Asian Grilled Corn

4 tablespoons (55 g) unsalted butter, at room temperature

2 tablespoons white miso

2 garlic cloves, finely grated

¼ teaspoon red pepper flakes

Kosher salt and freshly ground black pepper

Spiced Furikake (page 95) or store-bought furikake, for topping

While the corn is grilling, in a bowl, cream together the butter and miso with a fork. Add the garlic, red pepper flakes, a pinch of salt, and a few grinds of black pepper, mashing to combine. Spread the miso butter onto the cooked corn and sprinkle with furikake to finish.

Greek Grilled Corn

½ cup (125 g) Whipped Herby Feta (page 221)

¼ cup (38 g) crumbled feta cheese

½ medium red onion, minced

2 tablespoons chopped parsley leaves

Using a brush or spoon, slather the whipped feta onto the cooked corn to coat. Sprinkle with the crumbled feta, red onions, and parsley to finish.

BLISTERED MINI PEPPERS PANZANELLA

SERVES 4

Neutral oil (such as canola or avocado oil), for brushing

1 pound (455 g) sweet mini peppers

½ stale loaf country-style bread (about 12 ounces/ 340 g), cut into 1-inch-thick (2.5 cm) slices

¼ cup (60 ml) plus 1 tablespoon extra-virgin olive oil

Kosher salt and freshly ground black pepper

2 tablespoons sherry vinegar

½ teaspoon honey

2 garlic cloves, finely grated

½ medium red onion, thinly sliced

2 tablespoons drained capers

One 8-ounce (225 g) ball fresh mozzarella, torn into bite-size pieces

¼ cup (10 g) torn basil leaves

Peppers have an amazing ability to transform completely on the grill. They become sweet and jammy, making them the star of this bread salad. I like to grill mini peppers since they don't need cutting or seeding—an ideal choice for a laid-back cookout. Full-size bell peppers work, too; remember to core, seed, and slice them into quarters.

Prepare a fire for medium-high heat (see page 20), set a grate over it, and brush the grate with neutral oil.

Place the mini peppers and bread slices on a sheet pan. Using your hands, toss the peppers and bread to coat with ¼ cup (60 ml) of the olive oil. Season with salt and black pepper.

Spread the peppers across the grill grates and grill, flipping occasionally, until they are blistered and blackened in spots and begin to soften, 5 to 8 minutes in total. Grill the bread until crispy and charred, 1 to 2 minutes per side. Transfer the peppers and bread back to the sheet pan to cool slightly.

In a large bowl, whisk together the vinegar, honey, garlic, and the remaining 1 tablespoon olive oil. Season with salt and black pepper. Add the peppers, red onions, and capers to the bowl. Tear the bread into bite-size pieces and add to the mixture, along with the mozzarella chunks and basil. Gently toss in the vinaigrette to coat, seasoning with more salt and black pepper as needed.

GRILLED KIELBASA AND **CABBAGE** WITH HARISSA OIL

SERVES 4

Neutral oil (such as canola or avocado oil), for brushing

¼ cup plus 2 tablespoons (90 ml) extra-virgin olive oil

2 tablespoons harissa paste

1 tablespoon fresh lemon juice

1 tablespoon honey

Kosher salt

One 12-ounce (340 g) kielbasa, quartered crosswise, then halved lengthwise

1 medium head green or Savoy cabbage, cut through the core into 2-inch-thick (5 cm) wedges

Freshly ground black pepper

1 cup (240 g) sour cream

½ cup (25 g) coarsely chopped fresh dill

Grilled sausage lovers, this one's for you. Smoky kielbasa is paired with charred-yet-still-crisp cabbage, all drizzled with a spiced harissa oil. By cutting the cabbage through the core, you'll create wedges that hold together nicely on the grill. Don't be shy about showering on dill at the end—the herb brings some freshness to the plate.

Prepare a fire for medium-high heat (see page 20), set a grate over it, and brush the grate with neutral oil.

In a small bowl, whisk together 3 tablespoons of the olive oil, the harissa, lemon juice, and honey. Season with salt.

Place the kielbasa and cabbage wedges on a sheet pan. Using your hands, toss the cabbage to coat with the remaining 3 tablespoons olive oil and season with salt and pepper.

Grill the cabbage wedges and kielbasa, turning halfway through, until the cabbage is crisp-tender and slightly wilted and both are charred, 7 to 10 minutes total. Transfer back to the sheet pan. Using a basting brush, coat the cabbage and kielbasa with the harissa oil.

Place the cabbage and kielbasa on a serving platter, drizzling any remaining harissa oil over. Top with the sour cream in one big dollop and scatter with the dill to finish.

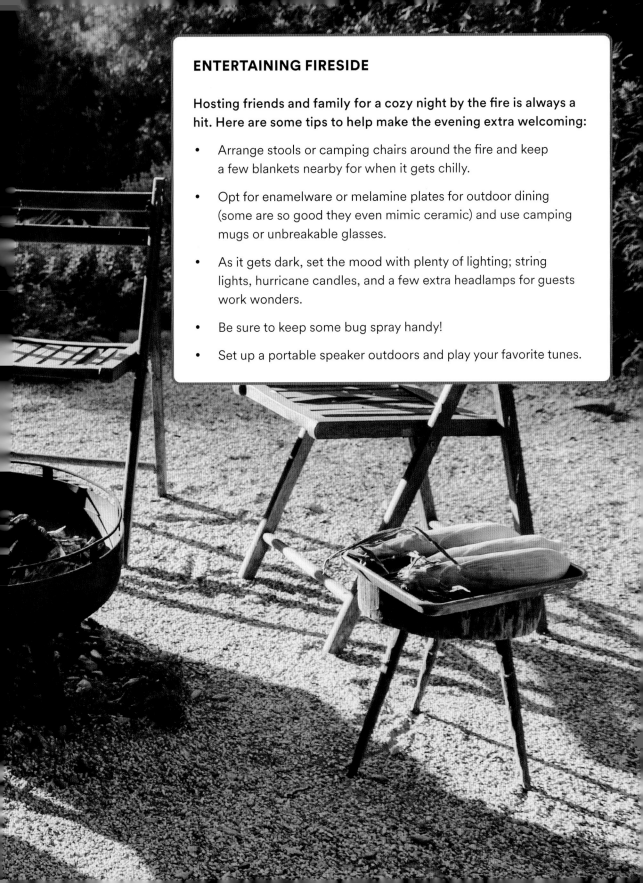

ENTERTAINING FIRESIDE

Hosting friends and family for a cozy night by the fire is always a hit. Here are some tips to help make the evening extra welcoming:

- Arrange stools or camping chairs around the fire and keep a few blankets nearby for when it gets chilly.

- Opt for enamelware or melamine plates for outdoor dining (some are so good they even mimic ceramic) and use camping mugs or unbreakable glasses.

- As it gets dark, set the mood with plenty of lighting; string lights, hurricane candles, and a few extra headlamps for guests work wonders.

- Be sure to keep some bug spray handy!

- Set up a portable speaker outdoors and play your favorite tunes.

Backyard Cookout

Here's the ultimate cookout menu with recipes that will easily feed a crowd. There's a mix of proteins for both meat lovers and vegetarians, and colorful veggie sides— and guests can have fun making their own s'mores for dessert.

GRILLED STONE FRUIT, TOMATOES
& SNAP PEAS WITH BURRATA
29

CHUNKY ZUCCHINI TOASTS WITH
WHIPPED HERBY FETA
30

JUICY LUCY LENTIL BURGER
113

GINGER-LIME PORK SKEWERS
142

S'MORGASBOARD
149

MUSHROOM AL PASTOR TACOS

SERVES 4

1 pound (455 g) mixed wild mushrooms, clusters or large mushrooms preferred (such as oyster, hen of the woods, or king trumpets)

1 medium pineapple (about 2 pounds/910 g), top and bottom removed, rind removed, cored, cut into quarters lengthwise

½ cup (120 ml) apple cider vinegar

¼ cup (60 ml) extra-virgin olive oil

2 chipotle peppers in adobo, plus 2 teaspoons adobo sauce

8 garlic cloves, peeled and smashed

2 teaspoons ancho chile powder

2 teaspoons ground cumin

2 teaspoons honey

2 teaspoons kosher salt, plus more to taste

Freshly ground black pepper

Neutral oil (such as canola or avocado oil), for brushing

12 corn tortillas

FOR SERVING

Chopped onions, chopped cilantro leaves, diced avocado, salsa, and lime wedges

Tacos al pastor, but make it vegetarian. Trust me when I say no one will be missing the pork in this mushroom version of al pastor. The secret? The mushrooms act like sponges for soaking up flavors from the citrusy, smoky marinade, and cooking them in clusters makes them super grill-friendly. Wild mushrooms are preferable for the best flavors and texture, but if you can't find them, portobellos will do; just be sure to remove the stems and gills. While your mushrooms are sizzling away, toss some pineapple on the grill until it turns caramelized and sweet—the perfect topping for your tacos.

To prepare the mushroom clusters, trim the tough ends while keeping the mushrooms intact. You want to keep the mushroom clusters big enough to handle on the grill. If you're using king trumpets, slice lengthwise into ½-inch-thick (1.3 cm) planks.

Cut half of the pineapple (2 large wedges) into chunks and put them in a blender or food processor. Add the vinegar, olive oil, chipotle peppers, adobo sauce, garlic, ancho powder, cumin, honey, and salt and blend until smooth. Season with additional salt if needed and black pepper to taste. Reserve ½ cup (120 ml) of the marinade for basting.

Pour the remaining marinade into a large bowl. Add the mushrooms and gently toss to coat. Let marinate for 15 minutes. Try not to let marinate longer than 1 hour or else the mushrooms will begin to lose their texture.

Prepare a fire for medium-high heat (see page 20), set a grate over it, and brush the grate with neutral oil.

Using tongs, remove the mushrooms from the marinade. Grill the mushrooms, turning once, until tender and lightly charred, 3 to 4 minutes per side. Brush with the reserved marinade while cooking. Grill the remaining two pineapple

wedges until charred and juicy, 2 to 3 minutes on each side. Transfer the mushrooms and pineapple wedges to a cutting board and let cool slightly. Slice the mushrooms and pineapple into bite-size pieces. Grill the tortillas until blistered, about 30 seconds on each side, immediately wrap them in a dish towel, and transfer to a basket or bowl. This helps them stay warm and soft.

To assemble: Fill the tortillas with mushrooms, pineapple chunks, and sprinklings of onion, cilantro, and avocado. Drizzle with salsa and serve with lime wedges.

SWEET & SPICY CHINESE CHICKEN WINGS

SERVES 4

½ cup (120 g) hoisin sauce

½ cup (120 g) ketchup

¼ cup (85 g) honey

¼ cup (60 ml) soy sauce

Juice of 2 limes

8 garlic cloves, finely grated

2-inch (5 cm) piece ginger, peeled and grated

2 teaspoons sesame oil

2 teaspoons five-spice powder

1 teaspoon red pepper flakes

3 pounds (1.4 kg) chicken wings, flats and drumettes separated if desired

Neutral oil (such as canola or avocado oil), for brushing

1 tablespoon toasted sesame seeds

2 scallions, thinly sliced

2 tablespoons chopped cilantro leaves

Lime wedges, for serving

These sticky, flavorful chicken wings pack a punch of bold, tangy heat, making them a finger-licking-good grill staple. Wings have a high ratio of skin to meat, which means more of the crispy skin we all love. The marinade for this recipe strikes a balance between aromatic Chinese five-spice, sweet hoisin sauce, and a touch of heat from red pepper flakes. And don't hesitate to grill the chicken until the skin reaches crispy perfection; the wings have plenty of fat to keep them moist.

In a large bowl, whisk together the hoisin sauce, ketchup, honey, soy sauce, lime juice, garlic, ginger, sesame oil, five-spice powder, and red pepper flakes. Set aside ½ cup (120 ml) of the marinade for basting. Add the chicken to the bowl with the remaining marinade and toss to coat. Let sit at room temperature to marinate for 15 minutes or cover and refrigerate up to overnight. Let come to room temperature for 15 minutes before grilling.

Prepare a fire for medium heat (see page 20), set a grate over it, and brush the grate with neutral oil.

Grill the chicken wings, flipping occasionally and brushing with the reserved marinade, until evenly charred and cooked through, 8 to 10 minutes if separated, 12 to 15 minutes if left whole. Test for doneness with an instant-read thermometer inserted in the center of a few wings to make sure they've reached a minimum of 165°F (74°C). If some pieces cook through before others, shift them to a cooler part of the grill.

Sprinkle the chicken with the sesame seeds, scallions, and cilantro. Serve with lime wedges for squeezing over.

SICHUAN-SPICED LAMB CHOPS WITH SESAME CUCUMBER SALAD

SERVES 4

FOR THE LAMB CHOPS

¾ cup (180 ml) extra-virgin olive oil

2 tablespoons ground cumin

1 tablespoon dark brown sugar

2 teaspoons five-spice powder

2 teaspoons ground Sichuan peppercorns

4 garlic cloves, finely grated

12 untrimmed lamb rib chops (about 3 pounds/1.4 kg)

Kosher salt

Neutral oil (such as canola or avocado oil), for brushing

FOR THE SESAME CUCUMBER SALAD

1 pound (455 g) seedless cucumbers like Persian or English, thinly sliced crosswise

2 teaspoons granulated sugar

¾ teaspoon kosher salt

2 tablespoons chopped cilantro leaves

1 tablespoon rice vinegar

1 teaspoon sesame oil

1 teaspoon soy sauce

1 garlic clove, finely grated

Red pepper flakes

Taking inspiration from classic Chinese cumin lamb stir-fry, this lamb chop rendition features a medley of aromatic spices plus the addition of five-spice powder and brown sugar that give it a delicious caramelized crust. Grilling these chops over an open flame imparts a charred, smoky flavor. To balance out the smoky richness of the meat, pair the chops with a crisp and refreshing sesame cucumber salad.

Marinate the lamb chops: In a small bowl, combine the olive oil, cumin, brown sugar, five-spice powder, Sichuan peppercorns, and garlic. Season both sides of the lamb chops with salt. Brush the spice mixture generously over the lamb chops to coat and transfer to a sheet pan. Let sit at room temperature for at least 20 minutes or cover and refrigerate for up to 12 hours.

Make the sesame cucumber salad: In another bowl, toss the cucumber slices with the granulated sugar and salt; let stand for 5 minutes. Add the cilantro, vinegar, sesame oil, soy sauce, and garlic, tossing to combine. Season with red pepper flakes. Keep chilled in the refrigerator until ready to serve.

Grill the lamb chops: Prepare a fire for medium-high heat (see page 20), set a grate over it, and brush the grate with neutral oil.

Grill the lamb chops, turning often to allow the fat to render, until a caramelized crust forms on the outside, 6 to 8 minutes, or until an instant-read thermometer inserted into the thickest part of a chop reaches 120°F (49°C) for medium-rare. Transfer the chops to a platter and let rest for 5 to 10 minutes. Serve the chops with cucumber salad alongside.

GRILLED HALLOUMI AND ARTICHOKE BURGERS

SERVES 4

Neutral oil (such as canola or avocado oil), for brushing

16 sweet mini peppers

Extra-virgin olive oil, for coating

Kosher salt and freshly ground black pepper

One 14.5-ounce (411 g) jar marinated artichoke hearts, preferably halves or wholes (large enough to fit on the grill grate without falling through), drained

One 8.8-ounce (250 g) block halloumi cheese, cut into 8 slices

4 brioche buns, split

½ cup (125 g) Any Greens Pesto (page 224) or store-bought pesto

Mayonnaise

Whether you're cooking for vegetarians or not, this burger is sure to win over all types of eaters. Grilling halloumi cheese for just a few minutes works magic, turning it crisp and golden on the outside and gooey in the center. Nestled into a pesto-smeared brioche bun, it's accompanied by zesty artichoke hearts (jarred ones work perfectly) and complemented by sweet, jammy peppers.

Prepare a fire for medium-high heat (see page 20), set a grate over it, and brush the grate with neutral oil.

Place the mini peppers on a sheet pan. Using your hands, toss the peppers to coat with olive oil, then season with salt and black pepper. Add the artichoke hearts to the pan. Add the halloumi slices to the same sheet pan and brush them with olive oil to coat on both sides.

Spread the peppers across the grill grates and grill, flipping occasionally, until the peppers are blistered and blackened in spots and begin to soften, 5 to 8 minutes total. Grill the artichokes until browned around the edges, 2 to 3 minutes total. If using whole artichoke hearts, press gently with a spatula to slightly flatten. Transfer back to the sheet pan.

Toast the brioche buns briefly on the grill until char marks appear, about 10 seconds. Lastly, grill the halloumi slices until golden, 2 to 3 minutes on each side. Grilling the halloumi last will ensure the cheese is warm and gooey for serving.

Spread the pesto generously over the bottom buns. Add the peppers, halloumi, and artichokes. Spread the top buns with mayonnaise and place onto the burgers to finish.

MEDITERRANEAN-STYLE GRILLED FISH

SERVES 4

Neutral oil (such as canola or avocado oil), for brushing

Two 1-pound (455 g) whole fish such as sea bass, branzino, or sea bream, gutted and scaled

Kosher salt and freshly ground black pepper

2 tablespoons extra-virgin olive oil, plus more for basting and drizzling

½ lemon, cut into rounds, plus wedges for serving

4 parsley sprigs, plus chopped parsley leaves for garnish

5 rosemary sprigs

1 pint (290 g) cherry or grape tomatoes, whole or halved if large

Flaky sea salt

Grilling whole fish over a fire until the skin is crispy, while basting it with rosemary branches dipped in olive oil—there's nothing simpler or more delicious. Two tips ensure success: pat the fish dry for crispy skin, and oil the grate well to prevent sticking. For extra flavor, top with smoky Walnut Romesco Sauce (page 40) and serve with Greek Lemony Foil Packet Potatoes (page 80) for a complete meal.

Prepare a fire for medium-high heat (see page 20), set a grate over it, and brush the grate with neutral oil.

About 30 minutes before grilling, remove the fish from the refrigerator and let it come to room temperature. Pat the fish dry with paper towels. Season inside and out with kosher salt and pepper. Brush each fish all over with 1 tablespoon of the olive oil. Stuff each fish with a few lemon slices, 2 sprigs of parsley, and 2 sprigs of rosemary (reserve the longest sprig for basting).

Place the fish onto the grates and grill until the bottoms are browned and crispy, 5 to 7 minutes, occasionally basting them with the reserved rosemary sprig dipped in olive oil. Using two metal spatulas, gently try to lift the fish from below. If they resist, allow them to cook a minute longer and try again, until they lift easily from the grill. Flip onto the other side and cook until an instant-read thermometer inserted into the thickest part of the fish registers 135°F (57°C), 5 to 7 minutes longer. If the skin begins to char too quickly, transfer the fish to the cooler side of the grill to finish cooking.

Transfer the fish to a large serving platter and top with the tomatoes. Drizzle with more olive oil and sprinkle with flaky salt and the chopped parsley. Serve with lemon wedges.

KOREAN KALBI-STYLE STEAK LETTUCE WRAPS

1 medium Asian pear (or Bosc pear), peeled and grated

½ cup (120 ml) soy sauce

4 garlic cloves, finely grated

One 1-inch (2.5 cm) piece ginger, finely grated

2 tablespoons dark brown sugar

2 teaspoons toasted sesame oil

1 scallion, thinly sliced

Freshly ground black pepper

1½ pounds (680 g) boneless rib-eye steaks

Neutral oil (such as canola or avocado oil), for brushing

Flaky sea salt

FOR SERVING

Kimchi, thinly sliced garlic, sliced scallions, and romaine lettuce leaves

Taking a cue from Korean barbecue, work some kalbi-style magic on your steak. The secret to achieving melt-in-your-mouth deliciousness is the Asian pear in the marinade, which works wonders to tenderize the meat. Serve the steak family-style alongside store-bought kimchi and crisp romaine lettuce leaves for tableside wrapping.

In a large bowl, mix the pear, soy sauce, garlic, ginger, brown sugar, sesame oil, and sliced scallion until combined. Season the marinade with a few grinds of pepper. Add the steaks to the marinade and toss to coat, pressing down to submerge. Cover and refrigerate for at least 30 minutes and up to 3 hours. Let come to room temperature for 15 minutes before grilling.

Prepare a fire for medium-high heat (see page 20), set a grate over it, and brush the grate with neutral oil.

Remove the steaks from the marinade. Grill the steaks, turning once, until lightly charred on the outside and medium-rare (an instant-read thermometer inserted into the thickest part of the steak should register 130°F/54°C), 6 to 8 minutes per side. Transfer the steaks to a cutting board and let rest for 10 minutes.

Slice the steaks against the grain into ¼-inch (64 mm) strips, then again crosswise into bite-size chunks; transfer to a platter. Sprinkle with flaky salt to finish.

Serve the steak alongside bowls of kimchi, sliced garlic, sliced scallions, and romaine lettuce leaves and have your guests assemble their own wraps.

SKIRT STEAK
WITH **CHIMICHURRI**
AND **HERBY SALAD**

SERVES 4

Ingredients continue

FOR THE CHIMICHURRI

1 cup (50 g) chopped parsley leaves (about ½ bunch)

⅓ cup (80 ml) red wine vinegar

⅓ cup (80 ml) extra-virgin olive oil, plus more for storing

½ shallot, finely chopped

1 small red chile (Fresno or red jalapeño), stem and seeds discarded, finely chopped

4 garlic cloves, finely grated

1½ teaspoons kosher salt

¼ teaspoon freshly ground black pepper

FOR THE STEAK

1 pound (455 g) skirt steak, patted dry

1½ teaspoons kosher salt

Neutral oil (such as canola or avocado oil), for brushing

Flaky sea salt

FOR THE HERBY SALAD

1 garlic clove, finely grated

2 tablespoons red wine vinegar

Here is a laid-back steak recipe perfect for grilling around the firepit with friends. The steak is thin, cooks up fast, and won't break the bank, plus it has that satisfying chewy texture we all enjoy. After a short time marinating in a bright, herbaceous chimichurri, your steak is ready to hit the grill. Slicing it thin after it rests makes it ideal for sharing. Mix some leftover parsley from the chimichurri with other tender herbs for a zesty salad that complements the richness of the steak— no leafy greens needed.

Make the chimichurri: In a bowl, whisk together the parsley, vinegar, olive oil, shallot, chile, garlic, kosher salt, and pepper. The chimichurri can be made up to 1 day ahead and stored in the refrigerator with a layer of olive oil on top to keep the herbs from browning.

Marinate the steak: Cut the steak crosswise into 3 pieces; this will make it easier to handle on the grill. Transfer to a shallow dish and season all over with the kosher salt. Pour half the chimichurri over the steak and rub until coated all over. Reserve the rest of the chimichurri for finishing. Let the steak marinate for 20 minutes at room temperature or up to 3 hours in the refrigerator.

Make the salad: In a large bowl, combine the garlic, vinegar, and mustard. Whisk in the olive oil in a slow, steady stream. The dressing should be on the acidic side and slightly mouth-puckering. Season with kosher salt and pepper and set aside.

Pick through the parsley and cilantro, trimming away thick stems and tough ends. Slice the remaining leaves and tender stems into 2-inch-long (5 cm) pieces and place in a serving

1 teaspoon Dijon mustard

⅓ cup (80 ml) extra-virgin olive oil

Kosher salt and freshly ground black pepper

½ bunch of parsley (about 1 cup/50 g)

½ bunch of cilantro (about 1 cup/50 g)

½ cup (25 g) dill sprigs, chopped

½ cup (20 g) basil or mint leaves, chopped

bowl along with the dill and basil. Cover and refrigerate until ready to serve.

Grill the steak: Prepare a fire for medium-high heat (see page 20), set a grate over it, and brush the grate with neutral oil.

Cook the steak pieces for 3 minutes, until char marks appear, then flip and cook for another 2 to 3 minutes. For medium-rare, an instant-read thermometer inserted into the thickest part should register 130°F (54°C). Transfer the steak to a cutting board and let rest for 5 minutes.

Slice the steak against the grain into thin strips. Transfer to a platter along with any juices from the board. Spoon the reserved chimichurri over the steak and season with flaky salt. Toss the herbs with the dressing and serve alongside the steak.

SMOKY SPATCHCOCKED CHICKEN WITH HERBY YOGURT DRIZZLE

SERVES 4 TO 6

One 3½-to-4-pound (1.6 to 1.8 kg) whole chicken

4 teaspoons kosher salt, plus more to taste

Freshly ground black pepper

1 tablespoon chili powder

2 teaspoons smoked paprika

2 teaspoons garlic powder

1 teaspoon onion powder

½ cup (120 g) plain yogurt

½ cup (30 g) mixed tender herbs (such as basil, cilantro, and dill)

1 tablespoon extra-virgin olive oil

3 garlic cloves

Juice of ½ lemon, plus wedges for serving

SPECIAL EQUIPMENT

Heavy-duty aluminum foil

Cooking a whole chicken over a fire can feel a little intimidating, but no worries—I've got some handy tips to help you get started. Be sure to give the chicken some time to dry brine for at least 8 hours, or even better 24 hours; this is the key to juicy chicken.

To ensure even cooking, you'll spatchcock the chicken by removing the backbone, allowing it to lie flat while cooking and resulting in extra-crispy skin. And here's the secret to achieving that sought-after smoky flavor and ensuring your chicken is tender and evenly cooked through: double-wrap the chicken in foil. You'll be rewarded with the most delicious, fire-kissed chicken.

Pat the chicken dry with paper towels. Place the chicken on a cutting board breast side down. Using sharp kitchen shears, hold the neck and cut along one side of the backbone, separating it from the ribs. Cut as close to the backbone as possible. Repeat on the other side to remove the backbone.

Flip the chicken breast side up. Using the heels of your hands, press down on the breastbone, flattening the chicken (you might hear a crack). Season the chicken all over with the salt and a few grinds of pepper, rubbing into the cavity, under the wings, and inside the legs. Place the chicken on a wire rack set over a rimmed sheet pan. Refrigerate, uncovered, for at least 8 hours and up to 24 hours.

Before grilling, remove the chicken from the refrigerator; let come to room temperature for about 20 minutes. In a bowl, stir together the chili powder, paprika, garlic powder, and onion powder. Lay out two sheets of foil large enough to wrap the entire chicken. Place the chicken on the foil and coat all over on both sides with the spice mixture. Wrap the chicken tightly in the two layers of foil and press to seal. This will help the chicken stay tender and prevent it from burning.

Prepare a fire for medium-high heat (see page 20) and set a grate over it. Since you'll be cooking for about an hour, remember to feed the fire with additional logs to maintain the heat while you're cooking.

Place the chicken onto the grate to cook. Check after the first 20 minutes by peeling back the foil to ensure that the chicken is cooking at a steady temperature. If needed, adjust the rack or spread out the coals to lower the temperature to keep the chicken skin from burning. Flip the chicken and continue cooking, turning occasionally, until it's cooked through and the internal temperature of the thickest part reaches 165°F (74°C), 55 to 65 minutes total. Transfer the chicken to a cutting board and let rest for 5 minutes.

Meanwhile, in a blender or food processor, combine the yogurt, herbs, olive oil, garlic, and lemon juice. Add a big pinch of salt and a few grinds of pepper and puree until smooth.

Carve the chicken and serve with lemon wedges and herby yogurt sauce to drizzle on the side.

GRILLED SESAME FLATBREAD

MAKES 8 FLATBREADS

1 cup (240 ml) warm water (110°–115°F/43°–46°C)

1 tablespoon active dry yeast

2 teaspoons kosher salt

1 teaspoon sugar

2½ cups (300 g) all-purpose flour, plus more for dusting

½ cup (60 g) whole wheat flour

Extra-virgin olive oil, for brushing the bowl and dough

Neutral oil (such as canola or avocado oil), for brushing the grates

2 tablespoons white sesame seeds

Flaky sea salt

NOTE: *If your kitchen is cold, try heating your oven to 150°F (66°C). Turn the oven off, place the dough inside, and keep the door slightly ajar to let it rise. Don't let it rise for longer than 5 hours, though; it will become tough and difficult to stretch. If you're going any longer, wrap it up and place it in the fridge.*

This flatbread is easy to master and grill-friendly, meaning it holds up without drooping on your grates while cooking. Cooking over fire creates blistered air pockets and a delightfully chewy texture. Whether you're dunking the flatbread into dips, enjoying it as an appetizer with some Charred Scallion Butter (page 225), or serving it as a side with Smoky Spatchcocked Chicken (page 67), it's sure to become a grilling staple.

Whisk together the warm water, yeast, kosher salt, and sugar in a large bowl or the bowl of a stand mixer. Let sit for 10 minutes for the yeast to activate and become foamy. Using a wooden spoon or the mixer with the dough hook on low speed, add the all-purpose flour and whole wheat flour, mixing just to combine and being careful not to overmix. The dough should feel slightly tacky and shaggy. Transfer the dough to a lightly oiled bowl, cover with a damp dish towel, and place in a warm spot to rise until it doubles in size (it should feel airy and pillowy to the touch), about an hour.

Prepare a fire for medium-high heat (see page 20), set a grate over it, and brush the grate with neutral oil.

Transfer the dough to a lightly floured surface. Divide the dough into 8 pieces, keeping them covered with a lightly damp dish towel while you work. Roll each piece into a 6-inch (15 cm) round (it doesn't need to be perfect) and transfer the rounds to lightly floured sheet pans. Let rest for 5 minutes. Brush each round on both sides with olive oil and sprinkle sesame seeds on the top. Place the rounds on the grill, sesame side up. When the breads begin to bubble up and brown underneath, 1 to 2 minutes, flip them over with a spatula. Once the second side is browned, about 1 minute, remove from the grill and set sesame side up. Sprinkle the flatbreads with flaky salt.

GRILLED HONEY PEACHES WITH YOGURT AND PISTACHIOS

SERVES 4

Neutral oil (such as canola or avocado oil), for brushing

¼ cup (85 g) honey, plus more for drizzling

1 tablespoon warm water

4 ripe peaches, halved and pitted

1 cup (240 g) Greek yogurt

2 tablespoons chopped roasted pistachios

Flaky sea salt

Mint leaves, for garnish

Ah, grilled peaches! There's nothing quite as satisfyingly simple as grilling ripe, in-season fruit. Topped with yogurt and pistachios, this warm-weather favorite becomes a "healthyish" dessert option that's hard to resist. Grilling caramelizes those ripe peaches, and basting them with honey as they cook brings out all their natural sweetness.

Prepare a fire for medium heat (see page 20), set a grate over it, and brush the grate with oil.

In a small bowl, combine the honey and warm water and stir to dilute the honey slightly.

Brush the cut sides of the peaches with some of the honey mixture and grill the peaches facedown, until the flesh is softened and char marks appear, 4 to 5 minutes. Continue basting the peaches with the honey mixture while cooking. Flip the peaches, basting and cooking until tender, 4 to 5 minutes more.

Place 2 peach halves in each of four bowls and top with a dollop of yogurt and ½ tablespoon of pistachios. Drizzle with more honey, sprinkle with flaky salt, and garnish with mint leaves.

FOIL
KETS

Foil packet meals are the ultimate hack for quick and easy cooking on the grill. It's a no-fuss, tasty way to prepare your food, whether you're at home or out camping. When you wrap your ingredients in foil, they cook in their own natural juices, which means they stay moist and flavorful. Plus, you can add your favorite herbs, spices, and seasonings, and they'll infuse right into the food.

The possibilities are endless when it comes to what you can make in a foil packet. Here you'll find seafood classics like Peel 'n' Eat Shrimp Scampi, vegetarian-friendly Miso-Butter Gnocchi and Mushrooms, and crowd-pleasers like Cheesy Pull-Apart Garlic Bread.

And perhaps the best part of foil packet meals? Once your meal is finished cooking, you can serve it directly from the packet, so there are fewer dishes to wash.

CHEESY PULL-APART GARLIC BREAD

SERVES 4 TO 6

8 tablespoons (115 g) unsalted butter, melted

2 garlic cloves, finely grated

2 tablespoons chopped parsley leaves

2 teaspoons thyme leaves

¾ teaspoon kosher salt

½ teaspoon freshly ground black pepper

1 loaf country-style bread

1 cup (115 g) shredded white Cheddar

1 cup (115 g) shredded mozzarella

SPECIAL EQUIPMENT

Heavy-duty aluminum foil

We all know what a hit garlic bread is with a crowd, and this version is a pull-apart cheesy loaf that makes the ultimate shareable appetizer. By slicing the bread in a crisscross pattern, you'll create nooks and crannies ideal for stuffing with Cheddar and mozzarella. The resulting bread has an epic cheese pull that guarantees each bite is a burst of garlicky, buttery deliciousness.

Prepare a fire for medium heat (see page 20) and set a grate over it.

In a bowl, combine the melted butter, garlic, parsley, thyme, salt, and pepper.

Slice the bread across the top in a 1-inch (2.5 cm) crosshatch pattern, cutting most of the way through but leaving the bottom intact. Brush the inner crevices with the butter mixture and coat all over the top and sides. Stuff the cheeses into all the crevices, and sprinkle some on top.

Wrap the loaf tightly in a layer of foil, making sure to seal completely to keep the cheese from oozing out while cooking. Place on the grill and let cook, flipping occasionally, until the bread is browned and the cheese is completely melted, 15 to 20 minutes. Peel back a corner of the foil to check for doneness and return to the grill if needed. Unwrap the foil and serve while still warm and melty.

GREEK LEMONY FOIL PACKET POTATOES

SERVES 4

¼ cup (60 ml) chicken or vegetable broth

¼ cup (60 ml) extra-virgin olive oil, plus more for greasing

⅓ cup (80 ml) fresh lemon juice

4 garlic cloves, finely grated

2 teaspoons dried oregano

1 teaspoon kosher salt, plus more to taste

2 pounds (910 g) medium Yukon Gold potatoes, cut into ¼-inch (64 mm) slices

Freshly ground black pepper

Lemon wedges

Flaky sea salt

SPECIAL EQUIPMENT

Heavy-duty aluminum foil

Foil packet cooking is ideal for outdoor settings; everything fits snugly into a pouch, cooking and steaming effortlessly. Marinating slices of potatoes in a lemon-infused broth before hitting the grill gives them a bright, tangy flavor and wonderful creamy texture. Serve them my favorite way—Mediterranean-style with an entire grilled fish—or alongside steak or chicken. Or on their own, swiped up with Easy Garlicky Aioli (page 223).

In a large bowl, whisk together the broth, olive oil, lemon juice, garlic, oregano, and kosher salt. Toss the potatoes in the liquid to coat, cover, and let marinate for at least 30 minutes and up to 2 hours in the refrigerator.

Prepare four large rectangles of aluminum foil, about 12 by 18 inches (30 by 45 cm). Brush each piece with olive oil.

Drain the bowl of potatoes, reserving ½ cup (120 ml) of the marinating liquid. Divide the potatoes evenly among the foil sheets, arranging a layer in the center of each. Drizzle 2 tablespoons of the reserved marinade over each layer of potatoes, being careful not to spill. Season with kosher salt and pepper. Bring the shorter edges of the foil to the center, then fold to make a seam in the center. Fold in the longer edges to seal and create a packet.

Prepare a fire for medium-high heat (see page 20) and set a grate over it.

Using tongs, place the foil packets seam side up onto the grate. Grill the foil packets without flipping (so you don't lose any juices), until the potatoes are fork-tender, 20 to 25 minutes.

Carefully open the foil packets, as hot steam will escape. Squeeze lemon wedges over the potatoes. Sprinkle with flaky salt to finish.

PEEL 'N' EAT SHRIMP SCAMPI FOIL PACKETS WITH **GARLIC BREAD**

SERVES 4

FOR THE SHRIMP

2 pounds (910 g) large or extra-large shell-on, head-on shrimp, deveined (see Note)

⅓ cup (20 g) chopped parsley leaves

¼ cup (60 ml) dry white wine

2 tablespoons extra-virgin olive oil

10 garlic cloves, minced

⅛ teaspoon red pepper flakes

Kosher salt and freshly ground black pepper

8 tablespoons (115 g) unsalted butter, cut into ½-inch (1.3 cm) cubes

Lemon wedges, for serving

FOR THE GARLIC BREAD

4 thick slices crusty sourdough bread

2 tablespoons extra-virgin olive oil

1 garlic clove

Flaky sea salt

SPECIAL EQUIPMENT

Heavy-duty aluminum foil

Old-school shrimp scampi heads outdoors, stuffed into foil packets for an effortless meal over the fire. Tender shrimp are simmered in a sauce of white wine and butter with loads of minced garlic. I like to use shell-on shrimp with the heads for this recipe; the shells keep them from overcooking, and the heads—well, if you haven't sucked on the oceanic, creamy heads of shrimp, this is your opportunity. If you only have access to shelled shrimp, they will work wonderfully, too.

While your shrimp are cooking away, grill the bread slices to make a side of garlic bread. Use it to swipe up any saucy remains.

Prepare a fire for medium-high heat (see page 20) and set a grate over it. Prepare four large rectangles of aluminum foil, about 12 by 18 inches (30 by 45 cm).

Make the shrimp: In a large bowl, stir together the shrimp, parsley, wine, olive oil, minced garlic, and red pepper flakes. Season with kosher salt and black pepper.

Divide the shrimp mixture evenly, spooning a mound into the center of each foil sheet. Top each mound with a few cubes of butter. Bring the shorter edges of the foil to the center, then fold to make a seam in the center. Fold in the longer edges to seal and create a packet.

Using tongs, place the foil packets seam side up on the grate. Grill until the shrimp are opaque and cooked through, 8 to 10 minutes. Don't flip these packets, as you don't want to lose any delicious juices.

Make the garlic bread: While the shrimp cook, brush the bread slices on both sides with the olive oil. Grill the bread slices until golden and charred, 1 to 2 minutes on each side. Transfer the shrimp scampi and toasts to a sheet pan.

NOTE: *To devein shrimp with the shells on, use kitchen shears or a small knife to cut through the back of each shell. Make a shallow slit along the flesh, then remove the dark vein with the knife tip.*

Finish the garlic bread: Rub the garlic clove against one side of each toast; the crisped edges will make it easy for the garlic to grate. Cut the toasts into halves. Sprinkle the toasts with flaky salt to finish. Serve the toasts alongside the shrimp scampi packets. Carefully open the foil packets, as hot steam will escape. Serve right away with lemon wedges.

SALMON FOIL PACKETS WITH CRUSHED OLIVES AND TOMATOES

SERVES 4

2 pints (24 ounces/680 g) grape or cherry tomatoes

1 cup (170 g) pitted Castelvetrano olives, crushed and torn into pieces

¼ cup (60 ml) olive oil, plus more for basting

¼ cup (15 g) chopped parsley leaves, plus more for garnish

4 garlic cloves, finely grated

2 tablespoons drained capers

1 lemon

Kosher salt and freshly ground black pepper

4 boneless salmon fillets (about 6 ounces/170 g each)

SPECIAL EQUIPMENT

Heavy-duty aluminum foil

It's not often that you can cook something that feels this elegant with so little effort. In this outdoor version of fish en papillote, foil ensures the salmon emerges flaky and tender every time. And to make this meal even better, there's a side of juicy, blistered tomatoes and briny crushed olives to really pack a flavor punch.

Prepare a fire for medium-high heat (see page 20) and set a grate over it. Prepare four large rectangles of aluminum foil, about 12 by 18 inches (30 by 45 cm).

In a bowl, toss together the tomatoes, olives, olive oil, parsley, garlic, and capers. Using a Microplane, zest the lemon over the mixture. Cut the lemon in half and squeeze the juice from one half into the mixture; stir to combine. Season with salt and pepper.

Divide the tomato and olive mixture evenly, spooning a mound in the center of each foil sheet. Top each pile with one fillet of salmon skin side down, baste with olive oil, and season with salt and pepper. Bring the shorter edges of the foil to the center, then fold to make a seam in the center. Fold in the longer edges to seal and create a packet.

Using tongs, place the foil packets seam side up on the grate. Grill until the salmon is opaque and cooked through, 16 to 20 minutes. Remove from the heat and carefully open the foil packets, as hot steam will escape. Serve with parsley to garnish and the remaining lemon half to squeeze over the salmon.

MISO-BUTTER GNOCCHI AND MUSHROOM FOIL PACKETS

SERVES 4

8 tablespoons (115 g) unsalted butter, at room temperature (see Note)

¼ cup (75 g) white miso

4 garlic cloves, finely grated

½ teaspoon red pepper flakes

One 17.6-ounce (500 g) package shelf-stable or refrigerated potato gnocchi

1 pound (455 g) mixed wild mushrooms (such as shiitake, oyster, or hen of the woods), tough stems trimmed, torn into bite-size chunks

2 tablespoons thyme leaves

¼ cup (60 ml) extra-virgin olive oil

Kosher salt and freshly ground black pepper

¼ cup (15 g) chopped parsley leaves

Grated Parmesan

SPECIAL EQUIPMENT

Heavy-duty aluminum foil

Shelf-stable gnocchi on the grill? Yes, and no need to boil water, either. The pasta pillows turn tender and crispy in foil packets with olive oil and umami-rich miso butter. Add earthy mushrooms, and soon you'll savor a comforting meal that tastes like it took all afternoon to make.

Prepare a fire for medium-high heat (see page 20) and set a grate over it. Prepare four large rectangles of aluminum foil, about 12 by 18 inches (30 by 45 cm).

In a bowl, cream together the butter and miso with a fork. Add the garlic and red pepper flakes, mashing to combine.

In a large bowl, combine the gnocchi, mushrooms, and thyme. Drizzle with the olive oil, season with salt and black pepper, and gently toss.

Divide the mushroom and gnocchi mixture evenly among the foil sheets, spooning a mound into the center of each. Finish each mound with a few dollops of the miso-butter mixture (about 3 tablespoons each). Bring the shorter edges of the foil to the center, then fold to make a seam in the center. Fold in the longer edges to seal and create a packet.

Using tongs, place the foil packets seam side up on the grate. Grill until the gnocchi and mushrooms are tender, 12 to 15 minutes.

Carefully open the foil packets, as hot steam will escape. Serve right away, topped with the parsley and Parmesan.

NOTE: *If your butter is cold and hard from the fridge, place it in a resealable silicone or plastic bag and smack it a few times with a rolling pin to flatten. This trick softens butter instantly.*

CHICKEN, CHORIZO, AND POTATO FOIL PACKETS

SERVES 4

1½ pounds (680 g) tiny baby potatoes, halved or thinly sliced if large, preferably Peewee

1 cup (230 g) Basic Tomato Sauce (page 222) or store-bought tomato sauce

6 ounces (170 g) Spanish chorizo or soppressata, cut into ½-inch (1.3 cm) chunks

1 red or yellow bell pepper, cored, seeded, and sliced into ½-inch (1.3 cm) strips

2 scallions, thinly sliced, green and white parts separated

5 garlic cloves, finely grated

3 tablespoons extra-virgin olive oil

½ teaspoon red pepper flakes

1 teaspoon kosher salt, plus more to taste

Freshly ground black pepper

1½ pounds (680 g) boneless, skinless chicken thighs, cut into 1½-inch (3.75 cm) pieces

2 teaspoons smoked paprika

¼ cup (15 g) chopped parsley leaves

Easy Garlicky Aioli (page 223), for serving

SPECIAL EQUIPMENT

Heavy-duty aluminum foil

Of all the ways to cook chicken, this might be the easiest. This Spanish-inspired foil packet has it all—paprika-spiced chicken, smoky chorizo, and a mixture of bell peppers and potatoes—making it a hearty, flavorful meal. Don't skip the garlicky aioli; its creaminess slathered over the potatoes is divine.

Prepare four large rectangles of aluminum foil, about 12 by 18 inches (30 by 45 cm).

In a large bowl, toss together the potatoes, tomato sauce, chorizo, bell pepper, scallion whites, half the garlic, 2 tablespoons of the olive oil, and the red pepper flakes. Generously season with salt and a few grinds of black pepper.

In another bowl, put the chicken, the remaining garlic, the remaining 1 tablespoon olive oil, the teaspoon of salt, a few grinds of black pepper, and the paprika. Toss to coat.

Divide the potato and bell pepper mixture evenly among the foil sheets, spooning a mound into the center of each. Place some of the chicken on each mound. Bring the shorter edges of the foil to the center, then fold to make a seam in the center. Fold in the longer edges to seal and create a packet. Let marinate for at least 30 minutes and up to 3 hours in the refrigerator until you are ready to grill.

Prepare a fire for medium-high heat (see page 20) and set a grate over it.

Using tongs, place the foil packets seam side up on the grate. Grill the foil packets, flipping occasionally, until the chicken is cooked through and the potatoes are fork-tender, 25 to 30 minutes.

Open the foil packets carefully, as hot steam will escape. Serve right away, garnished with the parsley and the reserved scallion greens. Pass the aioli at the table.

C
I

SKI

AST-
RON
LLET

You might have experience using a cast-iron skillet in your kitchen, but outdoors is where it really shines. It's a versatile workhorse that can fry eggs, whip up one-pan meals, and even bake desserts, all while imparting a unique crispiness to your food. Plus, on chilly evenings, cast iron retains heat remarkably well, keeping your food warm until you're ready to dig in.

Cooking with cast iron over a firepit is truly special; the pan evenly distributes heat, creates exceptional browning, and infuses a depth of flavor that's unmatched. These recipes are designed to showcase the versatility and charm of cast-iron cooking while serving up some tasty food. From appetizers like Drunken Prunes on Horseback to a hearty Fry-Up, sizzling Cowboy Steak with Gochujang Chile Butter, and more, the cast-iron skillet is your trusty companion for creating unforgettable meals.

Cast-iron cleanup is a breeze, too, thanks to its natural nonstick properties. Just give it a quick scrub with a brush, sponge, or chain-mail scrubber, dry it over some heat, and slick it with oil until next time.

CRISPY CHICKPEAS AND SHISHITO PEPPERS

An irresistible fireside snack that you'll want to grab by the handful, this finger-food sensation combines crispy chickpeas with sweet, blistered shishito peppers. Top it all off with a dusting of furikake for that extra umami flavor. Pro tip: make sure to thoroughly dry the chickpeas before frying to take the crunch factor to the next level.

SERVES 4

One 15-ounce (425 g) can chickpeas, drained and rinsed

4 tablespoons (60 ml) canola or vegetable oil

Flaky sea salt

8 ounces (225 g) shishito peppers

Spiced Furikake (recipe follows) or store-bought furikake, for sprinkling

SPECIAL EQUIPMENT

10-inch (25 cm) cast-iron skillet

Prepare a fire for medium-high heat (see page 20) and set a grate over it.

Spread the chickpeas over a paper towel–lined plate and blot until dried. Transfer to a cast-iron skillet with 3 tablespoons of the oil, shaking the skillet to coat the chickpeas and spread them into a single layer. (Starting with the skillet off the heat keeps the chickpeas and oil from splattering.)

Set the skillet on the grate over the prepared fire. Use a spatula or slotted spoon to toss the chickpeas occasionally. Cook until brown and crispy on the outside and tender inside, 7 to 10 minutes. Transfer the finished chickpeas to a paper towel–lined serving platter. Season with flaky salt. Discard the paper towel.

Let the skillet cool down slightly, then wipe it out with a dry paper towel. Place the skillet on the grate and add the remaining 1 tablespoon oil. Add the shishito peppers in a single layer and cook without disturbing until blistered underneath, 3 to 4 minutes. Flip with tongs and cook until blistered and tender, another 1 to 2 minutes. Add to the bowl with the chickpeas, season with flaky salt, and toss to combine. Sprinkle with furikake to finish.

MAKES ¼ CUP (30 G)

Spiced Furikake

2 tablespoons toasted sesame seeds

¼ teaspoon kosher salt

¼ teaspoon sugar

Chile powder, such as gochugaru or chipotle

5 small seasoned nori sheets

Combine the sesame seeds, salt, sugar, and a generous pinch of chile powder in a mortar and pestle or spice grinder and grind until the seeds are partially ground. Cut the nori sheets into bite-size strips, place in a bowl, and toss with the spice mixture to combine. The furikake can be stored in a sealed jar in a cool, dark place for up to 2 months.

CHEESY CORN SCALLION FRITTERS

SERVES 4

3 ears corn, shucked

½ cup (55 g) shredded low-moisture mozzarella

2 scallions, white and green parts chopped, plus more for garnish

½ teaspoon kosher salt, plus more to taste

½ teaspoon sugar

Freshly ground black pepper

2 large eggs

¼ cup (30 g) all-purpose flour, plus more as needed

2 tablespoons fine-ground cornmeal

Neutral oil (such as canola or avocado oil), for frying

SPECIAL EQUIPMENT

10-inch (25 cm) cast-iron skillet

Taking inspiration from gooey Korean corn cheese, these fritters are loaded with sweet corn and stretchy mozzarella cheese. The key to making the best fritters is having just enough batter to hold everything together, allowing the main ingredients to shine. When you're frying on cast iron over open flames, use a smaller amount of oil to keep things manageable and prevent splattering. After a few batches of frying, you'll become a pro at skillfully dropping spoonfuls of batter into the sizzling skillet.

Stand a corncob in a large bowl and slice the kernels off, starting from halfway down the cob and rotating the cob to keep slicing. This helps keep the kernels from scattering. Flip the corncob over in the bowl and continue from the other end until all the kernels have been removed. Repeat with the remaining ears; you should have about 1½ cups (250 g) of kernels. Run the back of a butter knife down the cobs to release the "milk" from the cobs into the bowl.

Add the mozzarella, scallions, salt, sugar, and a few grinds of pepper to the bowl of corn, mixing to combine. Season with more salt and pepper as needed. Add the eggs, flour, and cornmeal, stirring to combine. The consistency should be chunky and wet, with very little liquid batter. Add more flour by the tablespoon if needed. Cover and place in the refrigerator until ready to cook. The batter can be made up to a day in advance.

Prepare a fire for medium heat (see page 20) and set a grate over it.

Heat 3 tablespoons oil in the cast-iron skillet, swirling to coat. Place onto the grate. Test by flicking a drop of water into the skillet: if you hear it sizzle, the skillet is ready. Using a tablespoon, add a few heaping tablespoons of batter (each almost the size of a golf ball) directly to the skillet, being careful not to crowd the pan, and gently press each mound with a spatula to flatten it into a disk. Fry until the bottoms are golden brown, about 1 minute. Flip and cook on the other side until golden and crispy, about 1 minute. Transfer the finished fritters to a paper towel–lined platter. Season with salt while hot.

Repeat with the remaining batter, adding more oil to the skillet as needed. If your pan becomes too hot and starts smoking, take it off the heat to cool off for a few minutes before starting a new batch. Sprinkle the fritters with scallions to finish. Serve immediately.

SKILLET PIZZA MARGHERITA

MAKES TWO 12-INCH (30 CM) PIZZAS

1 pound (455 g) Basic Pizza Dough (recipe follows) or store-bought dough, at room temperature

All-purpose flour, for dusting

Extra-virgin olive oil

½ cup (115 g) Basic Tomato Sauce (page 222) or store-bought tomato sauce

6 ounces (170 g) fresh mozzarella, cut into 12 slices

8 fresh basil leaves

SPECIAL EQUIPMENT

12-inch (30 cm) cast-iron skillet

One of the best things about cooking pizza in a cast-iron pan is that the pan retains heat well, ensuring even cooking and a crispy crust. Start off with the classic margherita, and if you're throwing a pizza party, try some creative spin-offs from the recipes that follow. For larger gatherings, you can easily increase the quantities of dough and toppings.

Divide the pizza dough in half and form each portion into a ball. Place one ball of dough on a lightly floured work surface. Use your hands or a rolling pin to flatten it into a round. Drape the dough over the backs of your hands and gently stretch until it is about 12 inches (30 cm) in diameter. Place on a sheet pan. Repeat with the remaining dough ball and place it on a second sheet pan. Cover both rounds loosely with plastic wrap and set aside at room temperature until ready to use, for up to 4 hours.

Prepare a fire for medium-high heat (see page 20) and set a grate over it.

Brush the cast-iron skillet with olive oil, coating the inside of the pan. Transfer a pizza dough round to the skillet, using your fingers to press the dough toward the sides of the pan, forming a thicker crust edge.

Place the pan on the grate, using a spatula to press the dough toward the edges if it shrinks. Cook until you see bubbles forming on top and the underside has lightly browned (you'll return the crust to the heat later to finish cooking), rotating the skillet as needed to cook evenly, 3 to 5 minutes. Brush the crust with oil, then use two spatulas to flip it over and cook the second side until deep golden brown underneath, 2 to 4 minutes. Remove the skillet from the heat.

Recipe continues

Flip the dough once more so the darker side is facing up. Spread ¼ cup (60 g) of the tomato sauce over the pizza, leaving a border around the edge. Top with 6 slices of mozzarella and 4 torn basil leaves. Place the skillet back over the heat, cooking until the bottom is browned and the mozzarella has melted, 1 to 2 minutes. Drizzle with olive oil to finish. Repeat with the remaining pizza dough and toppings. Transfer the pizzas to a cutting board, cut into wedges, and serve.

VARIATIONS

Follow the pizza recipe above, replacing the tomato sauce and cheese with these specialty toppings:

Pistachio and Mortadella Pizza

Make the pistachio pesto: Place **½ cup (75 g) pistachios, ½ cup (120 ml) olive oil, ¼ cup (25 g) grated Parmesan,** and **2 tablespoons water** in a food processor and puree until blended, adding a splash more water if needed to loosen. Season with **kosher salt** and **freshly ground black pepper** to taste.

Cook the pizza as above. When the crust is done, top it with ¼ cup (50 g) of the pistachio pesto, **¼ cup (30 g) shredded mozzarella,** and **3 torn basil leaves**. Return the pan to the heat until the mozzarella melts and the pizza is done. Remove from the heat and finish with **dollops of fresh burrata, 5 thin slices of mortadella,** and **1 tablespoon chopped pistachios.** Drizzle with **olive oil** and **flaky sea salt.**

Spicy Sausage and Arugula Pizza

Make the spicy tomato sauce: Place **½ cup (115 g) tomato pizza sauce** and **2 teaspoons Calabrian chile paste** in a bowl and whisk until combined.

Cook the pizza as above. When the crust is done, top it with ¼ cup (55 g) of the spicy tomato sauce, **⅓ cup (40 g) shredded mozzarella, ½ cup (95 g) cooked and crumbled mild Italian sausage, ½ cup (10 g) loosely packed arugula,** and **2 torn basil leaves**. Return the pan to the heat until the mozzarella melts and the pizza is done.

Chinese Sausage BBQ Pizza

Cook the pizza as above. When the crust is done, top it with **¼ cup (60 g) barbecue sauce, ⅓ cup (40 g) shredded mozzarella, ½ cup (110 g) cooked and sliced lap cheong (Chinese sausage), 1 sliced scallion,** and **2 tablespoons chopped cilantro leaves**. Return the pan to the heat until the mozzarella melts and the pizza is done.

Shroom Pizza

Make the red pepper sauce: Put **½ cup (110 g) jarred roasted red peppers** in a food processor or blender and puree until smooth. Season with **kosher salt** and **freshly ground black pepper** to taste.

Cook the pizza as above. When the crust is done, top it with ¼ cup (60 g) of the red pepper sauce, **⅓ cup (80 g) Sweet 'n' Jammy Caramelized Onions (page 227)** or **⅛ thinly sliced red onion, 4 ounces (115 g) sautéed wild mushrooms, 2 tablespoons crumbled goat cheese,** and **2 teaspoons thyme leaves**. Return the pan to the heat until the goat cheese melts and the pizza is done.

Basic Pizza Dough

**MAKES TWO 12-INCH
(30 CM) PIZZAS**

2½ cups (300 g) bread flour,
plus more for dusting

1 teaspoon kosher salt

1 cup (240 ml) warm water
(110°–115°F/43°–46°C)

1 teaspoon extra-virgin olive
oil, plus more for greasing

¾ teaspoon active dry yeast

NOTE: *If your kitchen is
cold, it can prevent the
yeast from rising as quickly.
Heat your oven to 150°F
(66°C). Turn the oven off,
place the dough inside,
keep the door slightly ajar,
and let the dough rise.
Don't let it rise for longer
than 5 hours, though; it will
become tough and difficult
to stretch. If you're going
any longer, wrap it up and
place it in the fridge.*

Making great pizza ultimately comes down to the crust. This
recipe opts for bread flour due to its higher gluten content.
The result? A dough that's wonderfully stretchy, making it less
prone to tearing as you shape your pizza rounds. You'll end
up with a soft and chewy pizza that crisps up golden on the
bottom. If you have any leftover dough, save it to make Garlic
Bread Twists (page 131) over the fire.

In a large bowl or the bowl of a stand mixer fitted with a
dough hook, combine the flour and salt.

In a small bowl, stir together the warm water, olive oil,
and yeast. Pour into the flour mixture and mix until well
combined, 5 to 7 minutes if mixing by hand or about
3 minutes with the dough hook. Scrape down the sides of
the bowl, and the dough hook, if using. Cover the bowl with
a damp dish towel and let the mixture rest for 15 minutes.
Knead the rested dough on a lightly floured surface for 3 to
4 minutes; it should feel sticky.

Transfer the dough to a large, lightly floured bowl, cover
with a damp dish towel, and let rest and rise at room
temperature until doubled, 3 to 4 hours (see Note). Divide
the dough into two balls and place into two lightly oiled
bowls. The dough is ready to use at this point, or it can be
wrapped in plastic wrap and refrigerated for up to 24 hours.
If refrigerated, allow to come to room temperature for
20 minutes before shaping.

DRUNKEN PRUNES
ON HORSEBACK

SERVES 4 TO 6

20 medium prunes, pitted (see Notes)

½ cup (120 ml) bourbon

4 ounces (115 g) soft, fresh goat cheese, at room temperature

10 slices bacon, cut into halves crosswise

Hot honey, for drizzling (see Notes)

SPECIAL EQUIPMENT

12-inch (30 cm) cast-iron skillet

NOTES: *If your prunes have pits, score a small slit lengthwise in each prune, being careful not to cut all the way through. Remove the pits and discard.*

If you don't have hot honey, try mixing regular honey with a few dashes of hot sauce for a spicy kick.

You might be familiar with devils on horseback, but have you met their boozier cousin? These are sweet and sticky prunes soaked in bourbon, then stuffed with creamy goat cheese and wrapped in smoky, crisp bacon. To ensure your bacon doesn't stick and gets evenly crispy, start it in a cold skillet.

Place the prunes in a bowl and pour the bourbon over them, making sure the prunes are submerged. Cover the bowl and let the prunes soak for at least 1 hour and up to overnight at room temperature. Remove the prunes from the bowl and pat them dry; discard the liquid.

Stuff each prune through its opening with goat cheese, then gently squeeze to seal. Wrap each prune with a bacon slice, covering the opening. Make sure the bacon ends overlap, then trim off any excess bacon. Set aside on a plate, covered, in the refrigerator until ready to cook.

Prepare a fire for medium heat (see page 20) and set a grate over it.

Place the wrapped prunes into a cast-iron skillet, seam side down, leaving space in between. Place the skillet on the grate and let the prunes cook undisturbed until the bottoms are browned and the prunes are warmed through, 3 to 4 minutes. This will seal the bacon. Gently flip over the prunes with a spatula to continue cooking. Continue flipping until all sides are crispy and browned, 2 to 3 minutes more, transferring the finished prunes to a paper towel–lined platter. Drizzle with hot honey to finish and serve warm.

UMAMIEST SHROOM TOASTS

SERVES 4

4 tablespoons (55 g) unsalted butter, at room temperature

1 tablespoon white miso paste

4 thick slices country bread

1 tablespoon extra-virgin olive oil, plus more for brushing

Kosher salt and freshly ground black pepper

1 pound (455 g) mixed wild mushrooms (such as shiitakes, maitakes, or oysters), tough ends trimmed, torn into bite-size pieces

2 garlic cloves, finely grated

1 tablespoon soy sauce

1 cup (245 g) fresh ricotta cheese, drained

4 egg yolks, to finish (optional)

¼ cup (15 g) chopped parsley leaves

Lemon wedges, for serving

SPECIAL EQUIPMENT

10-inch (25 cm) cast-iron skillet

Mushroom toast comes together quickly on the grill and makes for a great appetizer or light meal any time of day. By sautéing the mushrooms in a cast-iron skillet first, you allow them to release their juices, resulting in an extra-concentrated mushroomy flavor. To elevate the umami, cook the mushrooms in miso butter and finish them off with soy sauce. And if you're feeling extra decadent, top each toast with a raw egg yolk—opt for the best-quality eggs you can find.

Place the butter and miso in a bowl and mash together until well combined. Brush the bread slices with olive oil and season with salt and pepper. Set aside on a sheet pan.

Prepare a fire for medium-high heat (see page 20) and set a grate over it.

Heat the tablespoon of olive oil in the cast-iron skillet, swirling to coat. Add the mushrooms and cook, tossing occasionally, until they release their juices and their edges brown, 8 to 10 minutes. Add the miso butter and let it melt, tossing with the mushrooms to coat. Add the garlic and soy sauce, tossing to combine. Season with salt and a few grinds of pepper and cook for a minute more. Meanwhile, grill the bread slices until golden and charred, 1 to 2 minutes on each side. Remove from the heat and set aside.

Spread the toasts with ricotta and spoon the mushrooms and juices on top. Make an indentation in the center of each toast and top with an egg yolk, if desired. Sprinkle with the parsley and squeeze the lemon wedges over the top.

QUESO SKILLET FONDUE

SERVES 4

8 ounces (225 g) sharp yellow Cheddar cheese, coarsely grated

8 ounces (225 g) sharp white Cheddar cheese, coarsely grated

2 tablespoons cornstarch

1 cup (240 ml) Mexican beer, such as Modelo

2 garlic cloves, finely grated

¼ cup (35 g) chopped pickled jalapeño

½ teaspoon ground cumin

¼ teaspoon ground nutmeg

Kosher salt and freshly ground black pepper

¼ cup (60 g) sour cream

1 small Roma tomato, chopped

¼ cup (35 g) chopped red onion

½ fresh jalapeño, seeded and sliced, for garnish

2 tablespoons chopped cilantro leaves

FOR SERVING

Raw veggies, cooked baby potatoes, cooked chorizo slices, and tortilla chips

SPECIAL EQUIPMENT

10-inch (25 cm) cast-iron skillet

This queso version of fondue stays wonderfully melty, thanks to the heat-retaining cast-iron skillet. But the cheese cools down eventually, so don't waste any time—dive right in while it's warm. Make sure to shred your own cheese for the best melt factor. If you have odds and ends of cheese in your fridge, such as smoked Gouda, Gruyère, or Taleggio, try swapping them in for some of the Cheddar to add extra depth of flavor. You'll end up with a spiced, cheesy dip to share, ideal for dunking slices of smoked chorizo, veggies, and tortilla chips.

Prepare a fire for medium heat (see page 20) and set a grate over it.

In a large bowl, combine the cheeses with the cornstarch, tossing to coat thoroughly.

Place the cast-iron skillet on the grate. Put the beer and garlic in the pan and bring to a simmer. Slowly add the cheese mixture in small batches, stirring constantly to ensure a smooth consistency. Once all the cheese has melted, add the pickled jalapeño, cumin, and nutmeg. Season with salt and a few grinds of pepper. Continue stirring until the fondue has thickened. Remove from the heat.

Off the heat, top the fondue with the sour cream, tomatoes, onions, jalapeño slices, and cilantro. Serve immediately alongside the raw veggies, cooked potatoes and chorizo, and tortilla chips for dipping. Return the skillet briefly to the fire if the fondue needs to be rewarmed.

THE FRY-UP

SERVES 2

4 slices thick-cut bacon

4 breakfast sausage links

¾ cup (115 g) sliced baby bella mushrooms

5 ounces (140 g) cherry tomatoes on the vine

Kosher salt and freshly ground black pepper

One 13.7-ounce (390 g) can baked beans (preferably Heinz)

1 teaspoon Worcestershire sauce

2 large eggs

1 tablespoon chopped parsley leaves

Buttered toasts, for serving

SPECIAL EQUIPMENT

10-inch (25 cm) cast-iron skillet

The fry-up, also known as a full English breakfast, might just be the best way to start the day, with its variety of delicious components. From crispy bacon and juicy sausages to perfectly cooked eggs, baked beans, blistered tomatoes, and savory mushrooms, there's a little bit of everything in one meal. Sautéing your mushrooms and tomatoes in leftover bacon fat imparts a rich, smoky flavor. The eggs are gently simmered in the saucy baked beans, poaching them for an indulgent creaminess that is best mopped up by buttered toasts. After this meal you'll have all the energy you need to take a hike.

Prepare a fire for medium heat (see page 20) and set a grate over it.

Arrange the bacon in a single layer in the unheated cast-iron skillet, then set the pan on the grate. Cook until the bacon starts to brown underneath, 4 to 5 minutes. Use tongs to flip the bacon and continue to cook, flipping occasionally to prevent burning, until crispy, 4 to 5 minutes more. Transfer the bacon to a sheet pan, leaving the drippings in the skillet. Add the sausages to the skillet and cook until browned and cooked through, 3 to 4 minutes. Set aside on the same sheet pan.

Add the sliced mushrooms to one side of the skillet and the tomatoes to the other and cook in the leftover grease until the mushrooms are browned and the bottoms of the tomatoes have blistered, 2 to 3 minutes. Season with salt and pepper. Transfer to the sheet pan.

If your skillet is very hot at this point, remove it from the heat and set it aside to cool down for a minute or two, then return it to the grate.

Pour the baked beans and Worcestershire sauce into the skillet. Bring to a simmer, stirring occasionally. Create two dents in the bean mixture, leaving some space on the

sides to add the cooked ingredients, and crack the eggs into the dents. Cook the eggs until the whites are opaque and the yolks are runny, 5 to 8 minutes. Return the cooked ingredients to the skillet. Season with salt and pepper. Garnish with the parsley and serve with buttered toasts.

JUICY LUCY LENTIL BURGER

MAKES 4

½ cup (120 g) mayonnaise

2 tablespoons Sriracha hot chili sauce (or other hot sauce)

2 tablespoons sweet pickle relish

1 cup (120 g) toasted walnut pieces, cooled

½ cup (40 g) panko breadcrumbs

4 garlic cloves, coarsely chopped

2 teaspoons ground cumin

2 teaspoons kosher salt

1 teaspoon ground coriander

Freshly ground black pepper

1 cup (180 g) cooked green or brown lentils (see Note)

1 large egg plus 1 egg white

4 slices American cheese

3 tablespoons neutral oil (such as canola or avocado oil)

4 brioche burger buns, split

4 tablespoons (55 g) unsalted butter, melted

FOR SERVING

Tomato slices, Sweet 'n' Jammy Caramelized Onions (page 227) or sliced red onions, and shredded iceberg lettuce

SPECIAL EQUIPMENT

12-inch (30 cm) cast-iron skillet

Here's a vegetarian twist on the classic Minneapolis-style Juicy Lucy burger. What makes this burger extra special is the lentil-based patty that has a slice of cheese sealed in the center—this lets the burger char up crisp on the outside while staying gooey and moist in the center. When forming the patties, be sure to seal the edges completely so that the melted cheese stays inside while you're cooking.

In a small bowl, stir together the mayonnaise, chili sauce, and relish. Keep the spicy mayo covered and chilled until ready to serve.

In a food processor, combine the walnuts, panko, garlic, cumin, salt, coriander, and a few grinds of pepper. Process until finely ground. Add the lentils, egg, and egg white and pulse until just combined but chunky, leaving some lentils whole. The mixture will feel wet at first; set aside for 5 minutes to absorb and reach a moldable consistency.

Divide the lentil mixture into 4 equal portions, then halve each of those portions. Roll each portion into a ball using the palm of your hand, then flatten each into a disk about ¼ inch (64 mm) thick.

Add one slice of the cheese to the center of a patty, folding in the corners to avoid any cheese overhang. Place another patty on top of the cheese. Pinch the edges of the patties together to seal all the way around, checking to make sure none of the cheese is showing. Place the burger on a sheet pan. Repeat with the remaining patties, then cover the sheet pan and refrigerate until ready to grill. The burgers can be fully formed and refrigerated up to a day ahead.

Prepare a fire for medium-high heat (see page 20) and set a grate over it.

Recipe continues

Put the oil in the cast-iron skillet and swirl to coat. Place the skillet on the grate. Once the oil is shimmering, add the burgers and cook undisturbed until crisp and browned underneath, 3 to 5 minutes. Flip and cook on the other side until browned, 2 to 3 minutes more. Meanwhile, brush the insides of the burger buns with the butter and place the burger buns cut side down on the grate until lightly charred, about 10 seconds. Transfer the burgers and buns to a sheet pan.

Spread the insides of the buns generously with the spicy mayo sauce. Assemble the burgers with tomatoes, onions, and lettuce.

NOTE: *To cook lentils, bring ½ cup (105 g) dried lentils and 1½ cups (360 ml) water to a boil in a saucepan over high heat. Reduce to a simmer and cook until the lentils are tender but still hold their shape, 20 to 25 minutes. Drain any excess water and let cool before using.*

SKILLET SEAFOOD PAELLA

SERVES 4

¼ cup (60 ml) extra-virgin olive oil

6 ounces (170 g) firm white fish fillets (such as cod, halibut, or monkfish), cut into 1½-inch (3.75 cm) chunks

10 ounces (280 g) large shrimp, peeled and deveined, with tails left on

1½ teaspoons kosher salt, plus more to taste

Freshly ground black pepper

1 red bell pepper, cored, seeded, and diced

1 medium yellow onion, diced

4 garlic cloves, finely grated

2 Roma tomatoes, diced

1 teaspoon smoked paprika

1½ cups (285 g) paella rice, such as Bomba, Calasparra, Bahia, or Valencia

Pinch of saffron threads

3 cups (720 ml) clam juice or seafood stock, warmed

¼ cup (60 ml) water

15 mussels, cleaned

2 tablespoons chopped parsley leaves

Lemon wedges, for serving

Easy Garlicky Aioli (page 223), for serving

Ingredients continue

There's no other dish that says party time like seafood paella. This dish was created to be cooked over an open fire, unlocking those crispy bits of toasted rice called socarrat scraped up from the bottom of the pan. Don't worry if you don't have a paella pan; a cast-iron skillet works just as well for this recipe. Take your time building that fire; steady, even heat is the secret to the best results.

Prepare a fire for medium heat (see page 20) and set a grate over it. You'll start your cooking over medium heat, but you want the fire to gradually mellow out to ensure that your rice cooks evenly.

Place a cast-iron skillet on the grate, making sure it is level. If not, tucking a crumpled piece of foil under the pan to balance it out usually does the trick. Heat 2 tablespoons of the olive oil in the skillet, swirling to coat. Once the oil is shimmering, add the fish and shrimp and sear until the fish is opaque and the shrimp are pink and cooked through, 1 to 2 minutes on each side. Season with salt and black pepper. Transfer the seafood to a platter and set aside. Remove the skillet from the heat.

Add 2 more tablespoons of the olive oil to the skillet and place it back on the grate. Add the bell peppers, onions, and garlic and cook until the vegetables soften and the onions are translucent, 3 to 5 minutes. Toss in the tomatoes and paprika, stir, and cook for another 1 to 2 minutes. Season with salt and black pepper.

Add the rice and crumble the saffron into the skillet, stirring well to coat. Cook, stirring frequently, until the grains begin to turn translucent at the edges, 2 to 3 minutes.

Add the warm clam juice or seafood stock, water, and the 1½ teaspoons salt to the skillet, stirring to distribute the

12-inch (30 cm) cast-iron skillet or 13-inch (33 cm) paella pan

Heavy-duty aluminum foil

ingredients into an even layer. Don't stir the mixture going forward.

Depending on your heat, the paella will take 20 to 30 minutes to finish cooking. Watch the skillet; it should be bubbling on top. Rotate it as needed to cook evenly. Once most of the liquid has been absorbed, begin tasting the rice. When it's done, it should be tender with a firm bite. If the rice is still very firm, add another splash of water. Once most of the liquid has been absorbed, add the mussels to the skillet, tucking them into the rice. When the mussels begin to open, after 3 to 4 minutes, add the shrimp and fish. Discard any mussels that haven't opened.

When you're in the final stage of cooking, you'll begin to hear a crackling sound from the rice crust forming on the bottom of the pan. To check for doneness, use a fork to lift an edge of the rice. The bottom of the rice should be crisp and deep brown in color.

Remove the pan from the heat, cover with aluminum foil, and let rest for 10 minutes. Sprinkle the paella with the parsley and serve with lemon wedges and aioli on the side.

CRISPY SALMON WITH TANGY PEANUT SLAW

SERVES 4

¼ medium green cabbage (about 12 ounces/340 g), cored and shredded thin

10 ounces (280 g) grape tomatoes, halved, or quartered if large

½ jalapeño, seeded and diced

⅓ cup (15 g) chopped cilantro leaves

Juice of 1 lime, plus lime wedges for serving

1 tablespoon extra-virgin olive oil

1 teaspoon honey

¾ teaspoon kosher salt, plus more to taste

Four (4-ounce/115 g) skin-on salmon fillets, about 1¼ inches (3.2 cm) thick, patted dry

Freshly ground black pepper

¾ cup (105 g) chopped roasted salted peanuts

SPECIAL EQUIPMENT

12-inch (30 cm) cast-iron skillet

Starting your salmon in an unheated cast-iron pan is the secret to sought-after restaurant-worthy crispy skin. Salmon is naturally fatty, so letting it slowly render all of its fat will result in shatteringly crisp skin and tender flesh. Spend most of the time cooking the salmon on one side, then gently flip the fish and take the pan off the heat to let it finish cooking in the hot pan to a medium-rare finish.

In a large bowl, combine the cabbage, tomatoes, jalapeño, and cilantro. In a small bowl, whisk together the lime juice, olive oil, honey, and salt. Add to the cabbage mixture and toss to combine.

Prepare a fire for medium heat (see page 20) and set a grate over it.

Season the salmon fillets on all sides with salt. Place the fillets skin side down in the unheated cast-iron skillet. Place the skillet on the grate and cook undisturbed, pressing down on each fillet with a fish spatula to make sure the salmon skin is in contact with the skillet, until the salmon is at least three-quarters of the way cooked through and opaque, 10 to 12 minutes. Test a corner of a fillet with the spatula; if the skin is still sticking to the pan, let it cook longer. It's ready to flip once it's crispy and releases on its own.

Gently flip over the fillets, then remove the pan from the heat. Set the hot skillet aside to let the salmon continue to cook off the heat, until it is just cooked through, 1 to 3 minutes, depending on the thickness of your fillets. Finish the salmon with a few grinds of pepper. Use a fork to flake the fish slightly to check for doneness.

Stir the peanuts into the slaw. Serve the salmon skin side up atop the slaw with lime wedges for squeezing over.

PAN-SEARED PORK CHOPS WITH MAPLE CHILE BUTTER

SERVES 4

4 tablespoons (55 g) unsalted butter, at room temperature

2 tablespoons maple syrup

½ teaspoon kosher salt, plus more to taste

¼ teaspoon Aleppo pepper or red pepper flakes

2 bone-in pork rib chops (8 to 10 ounces/225 to 280 g each), about 1½ inches (3.75 cm) thick

Freshly ground black pepper

2 tablespoons neutral oil (such as canola or avocado oil)

6 sage sprigs

2 garlic cloves, smashed

Flaky sea salt

SPECIAL EQUIPMENT

12-inch (30 cm) cast-iron skillet

Continuously flipping these pork chops in the skillet is what gives them that deep, golden-brown crust we all love. And when you baste them with maple compound butter off the heat, it imparts a sweet and spicy finish. An added bonus is the crispy sage leaves that become candied in the pan at the end.

Put the butter, maple syrup, kosher salt, and Aleppo pepper in a bowl. Mash together with a fork until well combined. Season the pork chops all over with kosher salt and black pepper and place them on a sheet pan to come to room temperature for 30 minutes to 1 hour.

Prepare a fire for medium-high heat (see page 20) and set a grate over it.

Put the oil in the cast-iron skillet, swirling to coat. Place on the grate. Add the pork chops to the skillet and cook until the bottom side is golden brown, 1 to 2 minutes. Flip and cook on the other side for 1 minute, then repeat the process, turning every minute, until the chops are deep golden brown and an instant-read thermometer inserted into the thickest part registers 145°F (63°C), 10 to 12 minutes total.

Remove the skillet from the heat and add the sage and garlic. Using a spoon, add the maple chile butter to the skillet, tilting the skillet and spooning sizzling butter and drippings all over the pork chops. Transfer the chops to a serving platter to rest for 5 minutes.

Cut the meat away from the bone, then slice against the grain into ½-inch-thick (1.3 cm) pieces. Spoon the remaining melted butter, the garlic, and the crispy sage over the chops. Sprinkle with flaky salt and serve.

COWBOY STEAK WITH **GOCHUJANG** CHILE BUTTER

SERVES 3 TO 4

1 bone-in rib-eye steak (about 2 pounds/910 g), at least 1 inch (2.5 cm) thick, patted dry

Kosher salt and freshly ground black pepper

2 tablespoons neutral oil (such as canola or avocado oil)

2 garlic cloves, smashed

2 rosemary sprigs

¼ cup (55 g) Gochujang Chile Butter (page 226)

Flaky sea salt

SPECIAL EQUIPMENT

12-inch (30 cm) cast-iron skillet

Could anything be more rugged than cooking a rib-eye steak in a cast-iron skillet directly over a fire? Rib-eye is one of the best types of steak for pan-searing, which really brings out that rich, beefy flavor. This cut's incredible marbling—those thin white strips of fat—allows it to stay juicy and tender even when cooked over high heat. Finish off the dark, seasoned crust by basting it all over with sizzling chile butter, or try Charred Scallion Butter (page 225). Channel your inner cowboy with this dish.

Season the steak all over with kosher salt and pepper and place it on a sheet pan to come to room temperature for 30 minutes to 1 hour.

Prepare a fire for medium-high heat (see page 20) and set a grate over it.

Put the oil in the cast-iron skillet, swirling to coat. Place on the grate. Once the oil shimmers, add the steak. Sear the steak, flipping every 1 to 2 minutes, until a dark crust forms on both sides and the steak is still very rare, 5 to 6 minutes total.

Move the skillet to the cooler side of the grate, adjusting as needed to lower the heat to medium.

Flip the steak and cook for another 2 to 3 minutes, until the steak is browned and an instant-read thermometer inserted into the thickest part registers 130°F (54°C) for medium-rare, or to your desired doneness.

Remove the skillet from the heat and add the garlic and rosemary. Using a spoon, add the gochujang butter to the skillet, tilting the skillet and spooning the sizzling butter and drippings all over the steak. Transfer the steak to a cutting board to rest for 7 to 8 minutes.

Place the steak on a serving platter and spoon the remaining melted butter, the garlic, and the crispy rosemary over the top. Sprinkle with flaky salt and serve. To slice, cut the meat away from the bone, then slice against the grain into ½-inch-thick (1.3 cm) pieces.

GIANT CHOCO CHIP COOKIE

SERVES 6

8 tablespoons (115 g) unsalted butter, at room temperature, plus more for greasing the pan

½ cup (110 g) packed light brown sugar

⅓ cup (65 g) granulated sugar

1 large egg plus 1 large egg yolk, at room temperature

2 teaspoons vanilla extract

1 cup (125 g) all-purpose flour

½ teaspoon baking soda

¾ teaspoon kosher salt

5 ounces (140 g) bittersweet chocolate wafers (or coarsely chopped chocolate chunks)

Two 1.4-ounce (40 g) candy bars of your choice (such as Skor, Twix, or Snickers), chopped into bite-size chunks

Flaky sea salt

Vanilla ice cream, for serving

SPECIAL EQUIPMENT

10-inch (25 cm) cast-iron skillet

Heavy-duty aluminum foil

NOTE: *If you don't have an electric mixer, use a wooden spoon and bowl. Cream the sugars and butter before adding the other ingredients.*

If you've been to BJ's restaurants, you know their famous Pizookie. This over-the-fire version of the giant chocolate chip skillet cookie is studded with your favorite chocolate candy bar (a Skor bar is a great choice). Look for brown edges to know when the cookie is done. Serve warm and gooey, directly from the skillet, with spoons and scoops of vanilla ice cream to share.

In a large bowl, using an electric mixer, or in the bowl of a stand mixer fitted with the paddle attachment, cream the butter until smooth, 1 to 2 minutes. Gradually add the brown sugar and granulated sugar and beat until fluffy, about 3 minutes. Add the egg and egg yolk, one at a time, beating well after each addition, then add the vanilla. Continue mixing until the eggs are incorporated and the mixture resembles cake batter. Add the flour, baking soda, and kosher salt, mixing until just combined. Fold in the chocolate wafers. Set aside.

Prepare a fire for medium heat (see page 20) and set a grate over it.

Grease the inside of the cast-iron skillet with butter. Scrape the cookie dough into the skillet and smooth into an even layer. Press the candy bar pieces into the top and sprinkle with flaky salt.

Cover the skillet tightly with aluminum foil and cook for 20 to 25 minutes, until the edges are browned and the top is puffy (it will still look doughy). Remove from the heat with the foil still on and let sit for 30 minutes to finish cooking and cool down. The center of the cookie will continue cooking as it sits, but don't worry if some parts remain slightly doughy; they are equally delicious. Top with scoops of ice cream and serve warm from the skillet with spoons to share.

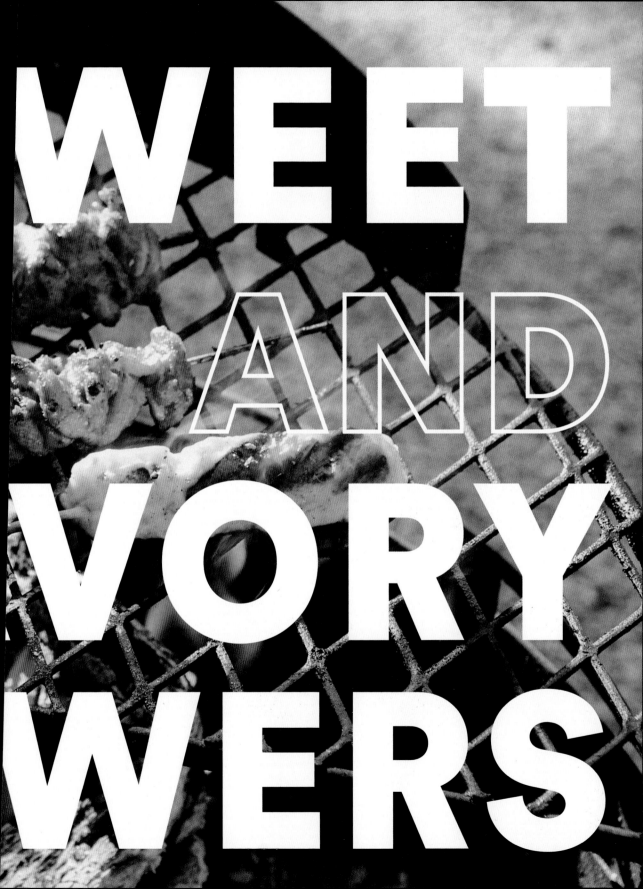

Most of the skewers from the backyard barbecues of my youth were shish kebabs with tough meat cubes and soggy veggies. Yet, when I reflect on the best skewers I've ever tasted, they were mostly from my travels—yes, we're talking about street-food skewers. What sets these skewers apart from the ones we make at home? The meat isn't just cut into chunks; it's also sliced into strips and folded accordion-style, creating pockets to hold the saucy marinade. The juiciest skewers feature cuts of meat with a high fat content that can withstand higher heat. That's why you'll be the star of the cookout with Chicken and Oyster Mushroom Satay slathered in sweet and spicy peanut sauce and Cumin Beef Skewers made from boneless short rib.

You can never go wrong with classic camp-out skewers like Piggies in a Blanket stuffed with juicy andouille sausage or Ginger-Lime Pork Skewers. For a sweet ending, indulge in churrofluffs paired with a mug of thick, dunkable Spanish-style hot chocolate.

To get started, invest in some metal skewers. Flat or two-pronged skewers work best and prevent your food from spinning all over the place. If you opt for bamboo skewers, be sure to soak them for a good 30 minutes before grilling—otherwise, they might burn or catch on fire, and you definitely don't want that.

GARLIC BREAD TWISTS

MAKES 8 TWISTS

1 pound (455 g) Basic Pizza Dough (page 103) or store-bought dough, at room temperature

All-purpose flour, for dusting

8 tablespoons (115 g) unsalted butter, melted

3 garlic cloves, minced

½ teaspoon kosher salt, plus more to taste

¼ cup (25 g) finely grated Parmesan

2 tablespoons chopped parsley leaves

Basic Tomato Sauce (page 222) or store-bought tomato sauce, for dipping

SPECIAL EQUIPMENT

Long metal roasting skewers, or wooden sticks cleaned and soaked in water for at least 30 minutes

For an interactive cooking experience, let guests forage for sticks to cook these garlicky bread twists. Use skewers or sticks that are long enough to hold a comfortable distance from the fire, and be sure to clean them well and soak your wooden sticks before using. If you're throwing a pizza party (see page 99), this is a wonderful way to use up any leftover dough.

Divide the dough into 8 balls. Place on a lightly floured sheet pan and cover loosely with a dampened dish towel. Stir together the melted butter, garlic, and salt in a small bowl.

Prepare a fire for cooking (see page 17). Allow the fire to simmer down, so the logs are mostly red-hot embers rather than roaring flames.

On a lightly floured surface, roll each ball into a 12-inch-long (30 cm) rope. Twist each piece around the end of a skewer or stick, tucking in the dough ends to secure. Brush with the garlic butter and season with salt.

Begin by roasting the skewers away from the flames, but in a spot that is still quite hot, about 12 inches (30 cm) from the embers, adjusting as needed to cook the dough evenly. Cook, rotating frequently, until golden brown and cooked through, 10 to 15 minutes.

Pull the twists to remove from the skewers and place on a platter. Brush the hot twists with garlic butter and sprinkle with the Parmesan and parsley. Serve with tomato sauce for dipping.

PIGGIES IN A BLANKET

MAKES 8 SKEWERS

¼ cup (60 g) whole-grain mustard

¼ cup (60 g) store-bought fig jam

One 8-ounce (226 g) can crescent roll dough

Four 12-ounce (340 g) fully cooked andouille pork sausages, cut crosswise into halves

SPECIAL EQUIPMENT
Long metal roasting skewers

Indulge in a classic comfort food that's as fun to make as it is to eat. This nostalgic crowd favorite is easily cooked over the open fire with just a few ingredients: smoky andouille sausages wrapped up in ready-made crescent roll dough, served alongside a sweet figgy mustard dipping sauce. These little piggies can be assembled on skewers and cooked by your guests; they'll be ready when they're golden brown and puffy.

Prepare a fire for cooking (see page 17). Allow the fire to simmer down, so the logs are mostly red-hot embers rather than roaring flames.

Stir together the mustard and fig jam in a small bowl. Set aside.

Separate the crescent dough into 8 triangles. Spread a thin layer of the figgy mustard sauce over each piece of dough and place a sausage horizontally over the point of the triangle. Roll the dough up so it is wrapped around the sausage and trim any excess dough. Skewer each one securely, piercing crosswise through the sausage.

Begin by roasting the skewers in a spot that is away from the flames but still quite hot, about 12 inches (30 cm) from the embers, adjusting as needed to cook the dough evenly. Cook, rotating frequently, until golden brown and cooked through, 5 to 10 minutes. Serve with the remaining figgy mustard dipping sauce.

GRILLED CHEESE SKEWERS WITH SPICY SPINACH-YOGURT SAUCE

MAKES 10 SKEWERS

1 cup (200 g) thawed and drained frozen chopped spinach, tightly packed

2 garlic cloves

One 1-inch (2.5 cm) piece ginger, peeled

½ green serrano chile, halved and seeded

3 tablespoons water

2 tablespoons plain yogurt

Juice of ½ lemon

¼ cup plus 1 tablespoon (75 ml) extra-virgin olive oil

1½ teaspoons ground cumin

1½ teaspoons garam masala

½ teaspoon kosher salt, plus more to taste

Neutral oil (such as canola or avocado oil), for brushing

12 ounces (340 g) paneer cheese (or other grilling cheese), patted dry, cut into 1-inch (2.5 cm) strips

SPECIAL EQUIPMENT

12-inch (30 cm) metal skewers, or bamboo skewers soaked in water for at least 30 minutes

Inspired by Indian saag paneer, this appetizer is made for outdoor grilling. Chunks of cheese are skewered and grilled until golden brown and gooey inside. These skewers are served over a spiced spinach-yogurt sauce, perfect for dipping with Grilled Sesame Flatbread (page 70). Experiment with cheeses that can endure high heat like halloumi, queso panela, or bread cheese.

Place the spinach, garlic, ginger, chile, water, yogurt, lemon juice, the 1 tablespoon (15 ml) olive oil, ½ teaspoon of the cumin, ½ teaspoon of the garam masala, and the salt in a food processor or blender. Blend until smooth but slightly chunky. Set aside until ready to serve, or make ahead and store in an airtight container in the refrigerator for up to 2 days.

Prepare a fire for medium-high heat (see page 20), set a grate over it, and brush the grate with neutral oil.

In a small bowl, whisk together the remaining ¼ cup (60 ml) olive oil with the remaining 1 teaspoon cumin and 1 teaspoon garam masala. Thread the cheese pieces on the skewers and place on a sheet pan. Brush the cheese on all sides with the spiced oil to coat. Sprinkle with salt to season (if using a saltier cheese, skip this step).

Cook the skewers, rotating them every few minutes, until evenly browned and slightly charred in places, 3 to 5 minutes total. Place them back on the sheet pan, brushing the skewers with the leftover spiced oil.

Spoon the spinach sauce over the bottom of a serving platter and top with the warm cheese skewers. Serve immediately.

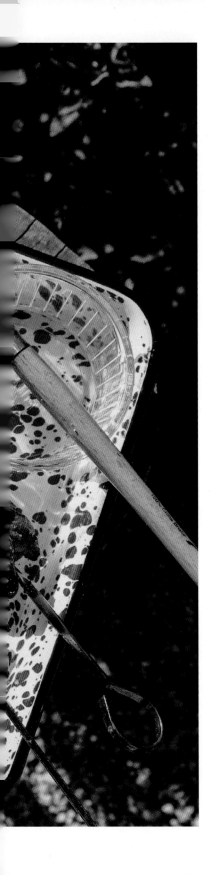

Street Food Party

Take a trip around the world with dishes inspired by the best street eats. Whether you're craving something spicy, sweet, or savory, there's a little something for everyone.

TAHINI CAESAR SALAD WITH
CRAGGY ZA'ATAR CROUTONS
33

SMOKY GRILLED CORN
41

GRILLED CHEESE SKEWERS WITH
SPICY SPINACH YOGURT SAUCE
134

CHICKEN AND OYSTER
MUSHROOM SATAY
138

CUMIN BEEF SKEWERS
145

CHURROFLUFFS WITH
HOT CHOCOLATE
146

CHICKEN AND OYSTER MUSHROOM SATAY

MAKES 12 SKEWERS

FOR THE PEANUT SAUCE

1 cup (240 ml) full-fat coconut milk

½ cup (125 g) smooth unsweetened peanut butter

2 tablespoons honey

Juice of ½ lime

1 tablespoon red curry paste

2 teaspoons soy sauce

1 teaspoon kosher salt

FOR THE SKEWERS

¾ cup (180 ml) full-fat coconut milk

2 tablespoons curry powder

2 tablespoons neutral oil (such as canola or avocado oil), plus more for brushing

1 tablespoon red curry paste

1 teaspoon honey

1 teaspoon kosher salt

1½ pounds (680 g) boneless, skinless chicken thighs

7 ounces (200 g) oyster mushrooms, torn into strips

FOR SERVING

Cilantro leaves, peanuts, and lime wedges

SPECIAL EQUIPMENT

12-inch (30 cm) metal skewers, or bamboo skewers soaked in water for at least 30 minutes

Juicy chicken skewers—marinated in aromatic spices and coconut milk, then grilled for a smoky char—are a street-food favorite you can enjoy in your own backyard. Served with velvety peanut sauce, each bite blends sweet and salty flavors with a hint of heat. For vegetarians, double the mushrooms and skewer them separately.

Make the peanut sauce: In a bowl, whisk together the 1 cup (240 ml) coconut milk, peanut butter, honey, lime juice, red curry paste, soy sauce, and salt. The sauce can be made ahead and stored in an airtight container in the refrigerator for up to 3 days.

Make the skewers: In a large bowl, whisk together the ¾ cup (180 ml) coconut milk, curry powder, oil, red curry paste, honey, and salt. Cut the chicken thighs into 1-inch-wide (2.5 cm) strips. Add the chicken and mushrooms to the bowl, gently tossing to coat with the marinade. Set aside to marinate for 20 minutes at room temperature or covered in the refrigerator for up to 3 hours.

Thread the mushrooms and chicken on the skewers, folding the strips back and forth accordion-style, alternating stacks of mushrooms between pieces of chicken. Leave a few inches on the ends for holding. Set the skewers on a sheet pan and season with salt.

Prepare a fire for medium-high heat (see page 20), set a grate over it, and brush the grate with oil.

Cook the skewers on the grill, turning occasionally and basting with the reserved marinade, until charred and cooked through, 10 to 14 minutes. Transfer to a serving platter and scatter chopped cilantro over the skewers. Sprinkle chopped peanuts over the peanut sauce and serve alongside the skewers with lime wedges for squeezing over.

LAMB KOFTA KEBABS

MAKES 8 SKEWERS

¼ yellow onion

1 pound (455 g) ground lamb

¼ cup (20 g) panko breadcrumbs

¼ cup (15 g) chopped parsley leaves, plus more for garnish

4 garlic cloves, finely grated

1½ teaspoons kosher salt

1 teaspoon ground coriander

1 teaspoon ground cumin

½ teaspoon ground cinnamon

½ teaspoon paprika

¼ teaspoon freshly ground black pepper

Neutral oil (such as canola or avocado oil), for brushing

Lemon wedges, for serving

1 cup (240 g) Lemony Yogurt Sauce (page 221), for serving

SPECIAL EQUIPMENT

12-inch (30 cm) metal skewers, or bamboo skewers soaked in water for at least 30 minutes

These kofta kebabs are crafted with spiced ground lamb, molded over skewers, and grilled until they're juicy and charred. Enjoy them as an appetizer dipped in Lemony Yogurt Sauce or turn them into a complete meal by adding shredded lettuce, sliced tomatoes, and red onion, all wrapped in a pita or Grilled Sesame Flatbread (page 70).

Using a standard box grater, grate the onion into a large bowl until you have about 3 tablespoons. Add the lamb, breadcrumbs, parsley, garlic, salt, coriander, cumin, cinnamon, paprika, and pepper and mix until well combined. Using dampened hands, divide the mixture into 8 balls.

Shape a ball around the tip of a skewer and roll on a cutting board, forming a 4-inch-long (10 cm) oval; repeat with the remaining skewers. Place the kebabs on a sheet pan. Cover and refrigerate for at least 30 minutes and up to overnight.

Prepare a fire for medium-high heat (see page 20), set a grate over it, and brush the grate with oil.

Cook the skewers on the grill, turning occasionally, until browned on all sides and cooked through, 6 to 8 minutes. Transfer to a platter and sprinkle with parsley. Serve warm alongside lemon wedges for squeezing and the Lemony Yogurt Sauce for dipping.

GINGER-LIME PORK SKEWERS

MAKES 12 SKEWERS

FOR THE NUOC CHAM SAUCE

⅓ cup (80 ml) water

2 tablespoons fish sauce

Juice of 1 lime

2 tablespoons sugar

1 garlic clove, finely grated

1 bird's eye chile, thinly sliced into rounds

FOR THE PORK

1½ pounds (680 g) boneless pork shoulder, fat trimmed

4 garlic cloves, finely grated

One 1-inch (2.5 cm) piece ginger, peeled and grated

2 tablespoons neutral oil (such as canola or avocado oil), plus more for brushing

Zest and juice of 1 lime

1 tablespoon fish sauce

1 tablespoon soy sauce

2 teaspoons sugar

1½ teaspoons kosher salt, plus more to taste

½ teaspoon ground cinnamon

Freshly ground black pepper

Inspired by Vietnamese grilled lemongrass pork, this marinade opts for readily available ginger and lime. These smoky, charred pork skewers pair wonderfully with lettuce wraps and an abundance of fresh herbs and veggies, adding a refreshing crunch. And don't forget the finishing touch: a dunk in bright and citrusy nuoc cham sauce.

Make the nuoc cham sauce: In a small bowl, whisk together the water, fish sauce, lime juice, and sugar until the sugar is dissolved. Stir in the garlic and chiles. The sauce can be made ahead and stored in an airtight container in the refrigerator for up to 3 days.

Make the pork: Place the pork on a plate and freeze until the meat is firm and partially frozen, about 1 hour.

Meanwhile, make the marinade. In a large bowl, whisk together the garlic, ginger, oil, lime zest and juice, fish sauce, soy sauce, sugar, salt, cinnamon, and a few grinds of pepper.

Slice the partially frozen pork against the grain into thin pieces about 1/8 inch (30 mm) thick. Cut them into strips about 1 inch (2.5 cm) wide, trimming out fat as necessary. Add the pork pieces to the large bowl and toss the meat to coat with the marinade. Cover and chill in the refrigerator for at least 1 hour and up to overnight.

Thread the pork on the skewers, folding the strips back and forth accordion-style. Leave a few inches on the ends for holding. Place the skewers on a sheet pan and season with salt. Keep loosely covered until ready to grill.

Prepare a fire for medium-high heat (see page 20), set a grate over it, and brush the grate with oil.

Torn mint leaves, shredded carrots, cucumber slices, crushed peanuts, and lettuce leaves for wrapping

12-inch (30 cm) metal skewers, or bamboo skewers soaked in water for at least 30 minutes

Cook the skewers on the grill, turning occasionally, until charred on all sides and cooked through, 9 to 11 minutes. Transfer the skewers to a serving platter and drizzle with a few spoonfuls of the nuoc cham sauce.

Serve the skewers alongside the mint, carrots, cucumber slices, peanuts, and lettuce leaves, and pass the remaining sauce for dipping.

CUMIN BEEF SKEWERS

MAKES 12 SKEWERS

FOR THE TAHINI–SOY SAUCE

½ cup (120 g) tahini, stirred

2 tablespoons soy sauce

1 tablespoon rice vinegar

2 teaspoons honey

1 garlic clove, finely grated

One 1-inch (2.5 cm) piece ginger, peeled and grated

Kosher salt

FOR THE BEEF

1½ pounds (680 g) boneless short ribs

¼ cup (60 ml) soy sauce

4 garlic cloves, finely grated

One 2-inch (5 cm) piece ginger, peeled and grated

2 tablespoons fish sauce

2 tablespoons light brown sugar

2 tablespoons neutral oil (such as canola or avocado oil), plus more for brushing

Juice of 1 lime, plus lime wedges for serving

1½ teaspoons ground cumin

Kosher salt

2 scallions, thinly sliced

SPECIAL EQUIPMENT

12-inch (30 cm) metal skewers, or bamboo skewers soaked in water for at least 30 minutes

For the best tender beef skewers, use boneless short ribs. They're marbled with fat, which gives them crispy edges when grilled. To round out your meal, serve them alongside your favorite salad.

Make the tahini-soy sauce: In a small bowl, whisk together the tahini, soy sauce, vinegar, honey, garlic, and ginger. Add water by the tablespoon to thin until the sauce reaches a runny but thick consistency. Season with salt to taste.

Make the beef: Place the short ribs on a plate and freeze until the meat is firm and partially frozen, about 30 minutes.

Meanwhile, make the marinade. In a large bowl, whisk together the soy sauce, garlic, ginger, fish sauce, brown sugar, oil, lime juice, and cumin.

Slice the partially frozen beef against the grain into thin pieces about ¼ inch (64 mm) thick. Cut them into strips about 1 inch (2.5 cm) wide, trimming out any tough gristly bits, and add to the large bowl, tossing in the marinade to combine. Cover and chill in the refrigerator for at least 1 hour and up to overnight.

Thread the beef on the skewers, folding the strips back and forth accordion-style. Leave a few inches on the ends for holding. Place the skewers on a sheet pan and season with salt. Keep loosely covered until ready to grill.

Prepare a fire for medium-high heat (see page 20), set a grate over it, and brush the grate with oil.

Cook the skewers on the grill, turning occasionally, until charred on all sides and cooked through, 5 to 6 minutes. Transfer the skewers to a serving platter and sprinkle with the scallions.

Serve with lime wedges for squeezing and tahini-soy sauce for dipping.

CHURROFLUFFS
WITH **HOT CHOCOLATE**

MAKES 8 SKEWERS

FOR THE HOT CHOCOLATE

4 cups (950 ml) milk or nondairy milk

¼ cup (50 g) sugar

1 teaspoon cornstarch

1 teaspoon vanilla extract

8 ounces (225 g) bittersweet chocolate (70% cacao), chopped

Ground cinnamon or cayenne pepper, for sprinkling

FOR THE CHURROFLUFFS

½ cup (100 g) sugar

1 tablespoon ground cinnamon

One 8-ounce (226 g) can crescent roll dough

8 tablespoons (115 g) unsalted butter, melted

Marshmallow Fluff, for spreading

SPECIAL EQUIPMENT

Long metal roasting skewers, or wooden sticks cleaned and soaked in water for at least 30 minutes

Here's a fun twist on churros: an on-a-stick version that uses store-bought crescent dough. And to make it even better, smear dollops of Marshmallow Fluff onto the finished churros and roast them briefly to finish. Pair with a decadent Spanish-style hot chocolate that's sippable and thick enough for dunking the warm churros.

Make the hot chocolate: Whisk together the milk, sugar, cornstarch, and vanilla in a saucepan over medium heat (on a stovetop or camping stove). Heat until the mixture steams, 2 to 3 minutes. Remove from the heat, add the chocolate, and whisk until melted and incorporated.

Make the churrofluffs: Stir together the sugar and cinnamon in a small bowl. Pour onto a shallow plate and set aside for the coating.

Prepare a fire for cooking (see page 17). Allow the fire to simmer down, so the logs are mostly red-hot embers rather than roaring flames.

Pop open the can of crescent rolls and separate the dough along the perforations. Wrap 8 dough triangles around roasting skewers or sticks, tucking in the loose ends to secure.

Begin by roasting the skewers in a spot that is away from the flames but still quite hot, about 12 inches (30 cm) from the embers, adjusting as needed to cook the dough evenly. Cook, rotating frequently, until golden brown and cooked through, 5 to 10 minutes. Brush the melted butter over the churros and roll them in the cinnamon-sugar mixture to coat. Spread the Marshmallow Fluff on top of each churro and roast over the fire until the marshmallow is browned in spots.

Rewarm the hot chocolate and ladle into mugs. Sprinkle with cinnamon or cayenne and serve alongside the churrofluffs.

S'MORGASBOARD

Gathering around a crackling fire and indulging in s'mores as the sky darkens is the perfect way to end an evening outdoors. This classic campfire dessert—made with gooey roasted marshmallows, rich chocolate, and crisp graham crackers—brings people together and creates long-lasting memories. The process of making s'mores is as delightful as eating them: roasting marshmallows to a golden brown or letting them get slightly burnt at the edges, then squishing them between layers of chocolate and graham crackers and savoring the warm, melty bliss.

While the traditional combination of graham crackers, chocolate, and marshmallows is always a hit, there are countless variations to explore. Why not set up a s'mores board and let everyone dive in and get creative with their favorite versions? You can experiment with different types of chocolate, such as milk, bittersweet, and white cookies 'n' creme bars. Or try spreads like Nutella and peanut butter for an extra layer of fun. Adding fresh strawberries and raspberries to the board will brighten the flavors. And don't forget to mix up the base: go beyond graham crackers with options like chocolate chip cookies, Samoas, Biscoff cookies, or even savory choices like ruffled potato chips and flat pretzels.

TO MAKE S'MORES, prepare a fire for cooking (see page 17). Allow the fire to simmer down, so the logs are mostly red-hot embers rather than roaring flames. Meanwhile, set out some long metal roasting skewers or gather and clean some wooden sticks and soak them for at least 30 minutes. Prepare your s'mores board and when the fire is ready, invite your guests to gather around the fire, roast their own marshmallows, and mix and match their own s'mores combinations.

OVER AND NDER OALS

Some things just get better when they're charred—and cooking over coals means you can get the high heat without smoking up your entire kitchen. Plus, there's no denying that cooking with hot coals makes you feel like a major badass. It's the ultimate minimalist approach to live-fire cooking, perfect for thrill-seekers who want to push the boundaries beyond standard cooking methods.

If you're just starting out, you might want to try burying a few Japanese sweet potatoes (see page 167) under your hot coals at the end of the night. After about an hour, they become incredibly tender and sweet inside. Feeling a bit adventurous? Give Ember-Roasted Leeks a try. There's something about letting them char completely, then peeling back the layers to reveal the most delicate, melt-in-your-mouth caramelized veggie, that feels like you've pulled off a culinary masterpiece. And for dessert, don't miss out on the camp classic Stuffed Banana Boats, loaded with all your favorite fillings.

When cooking on coals, the best results come from coals that are white-hot—they're super hot and ready to go. Don't fret if the ashes stick to your food; simply brush them off. I prefer using high-quality seasoned wood or lump charcoal when my food is in direct contact with the coals because it adds a fantastic flavor boost. So get those coals started!

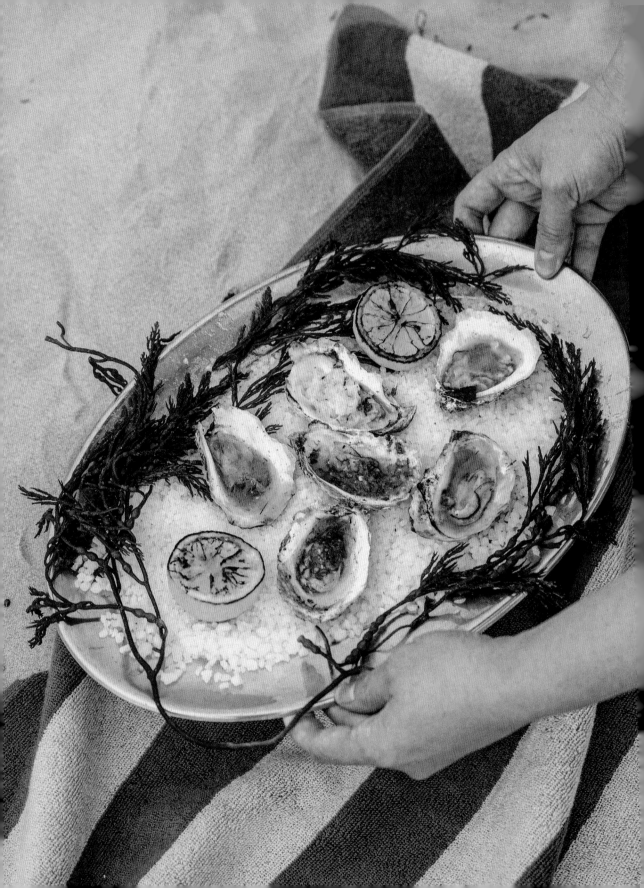

CREAMY LEEK GRILLED OYSTERS

SERVES 4

1 large leek, light green and white parts only, cut in half lengthwise, thinly sliced, and thoroughly rinsed

¼ cup (60 ml) dry white wine (such as sauvignon blanc or pinot grigio)

2 tablespoons unsalted butter

Kosher salt and freshly ground black pepper

⅓ cup (80 ml) heavy cream, plus more as needed

¼ cup (25 g) grated Parmesan

16 large oysters (such as Blue Points, Malpeque, and Wellfleet)

1 lemon, halved, fresh or grilled, for serving

SPECIAL EQUIPMENT

Oyster shucker

Coarse rock salt

West Coast–style grilled oysters are, in my opinion, the best way to enjoy our larger shelled friends. The technique is simple: adorned with a variety of toppings, these delicacies are gently poached in their own flavorful juices, resulting in a culinary experience like no other. Cooking them over coals gives them that irresistible smoky aroma, and the nooks and crannies of the coals make it easy to nestle the oysters right into place. Try them with creamy leeks or go ahead and get creative with your toppings (see Variations).

Place the leeks, wine, and butter in a small saucepan over medium-high heat, bring to a boil, then reduce the heat to a low simmer. Season with salt and a few grinds of pepper. Cook, stirring occasionally, until the leeks are very soft and nearly caramelized, 10 to 15 minutes. Stir in the cream and Parmesan and cook for another minute until thickened. Season to taste with salt. If the topping becomes too thick as it sits, loosen the mixture with another splash of heavy cream before using. Cover loosely and set aside until ready to use. Creamy leeks can be made up to 2 days in advance and stored in an airtight container in the refrigerator.

Meanwhile, shuck the oysters: Using a folded towel or shucking glove to protect your hand, place the oyster flat, cup side up, in your palm. Place the oyster shucker along the split opening of the shell. Gently insert and twist the blade. Once the shell splits open, move the shucker flat across the oyster and pull it open until half of the shell is off. Discard the empty shell. Scoop underneath the meat with the shucker to cut it loose from the other shell. Check for any shell pieces and discard them. Set the oyster back inside its shell, being careful not to lose any juices. Finish shucking the remaining oysters. Keep the oysters refrigerated on a platter until your coals are ready for cooking.

Prepare a wood fire or coals for cooking (see page 22) and allow the flames to die out until you have a nice bed of hot embers.

Top each oyster with about a teaspoon of creamy leeks. Place the oysters on the coals, nestling them securely into place, trying to keep all the juices inside. Cook until the liquid is bubbling around the edges, 1 to 2 minutes. Make sure not to overcook these; you want them to stay juicy. Transfer the oysters to a clean platter lined with rock salt and serve warm with lemon halves for squeezing over.

VARIATIONS

Pesto

Top the oysters with small dollops of Any Greens Pesto (page 224) in place of the creamy leeks.

Chile Butter

Finish the cooked oysters with pats of Gochujang Chile Butter (page 226).

Seafood Feast

Get ready to dive into a seafood feast bursting with bright, fresh flavors. Slurp up some oysters and dig into a whole grilled fish—it's a seafood lover's dream come true.

CREAMY LEEK GRILLED OYSTERS
155

CUMIN GRILLED CARROTS WITH LEMONY YOGURT
37

MEDITERRANEAN-STYLE GRILLED FISH
60

GRILLED HONEY PEACHES WITH YOGURT AND PISTACHIOS
73

COAL-ROASTED CHEESE WRAPPED IN CABBAGE LEAVES

SERVES 4

4 to 6 red or green cabbage leaves

10-ounce (280 g) wheel of Brie or Camembert (or other soft cheese with an edible rind)

1 tablespoon honey

¼ teaspoon red pepper flakes

2 teaspoons chopped fresh tender herbs (such as thyme, sage, or dill)

1 baguette, sliced

Fresh fruit, for serving

SPECIAL EQUIPMENT

4 long bamboo skewers soaked in water for at least 30 minutes

A wheel of creamy cheese in hearty cabbage leaves, buried under a bed of hot coals, makes for an impressive appetizer or dessert. Once it's unearthed, you'll have the most decadent gooey cheese for dipping and spreading over crusty baguette slices.

Prepare a wood fire or coals for cooking (see page 22) and allow the flames to die out until you have a nice bed of hot embers.

Trim off the tough bottom stems of the cabbage leaves. This will make the leaves more pliable for wrapping. Slice the cheese in half horizontally. Spread the honey on the exposed creamy interior of both halves and sprinkle with the red pepper flakes and herbs. Press the two halves together. Wrap the cheese with the cabbage leaves, covering the cheese entirely, and secure with skewers. Make sure the wheel is well wrapped so that the cheese doesn't leak while cooking.

Spread the hot coals, completely bury the wheel under the coals, and cook for 10 minutes. Using a shovel or tongs, pull the wheel from the coals and place on a serving platter. Let it cool slightly and unwrap the cabbage leaves. Serve immediately with the baguette slices and fruit while still warm and gooey.

SMOKIEST BABA GHANOUSH

MAKES ABOUT 2 CUPS (450 G)

1 medium globe eggplant (about 1 pound/455 g)

¼ cup (60 g) tahini, stirred smooth

2 garlic cloves, finely grated

2 tablespoons fresh lemon juice

½ teaspoon kosher salt, plus more to taste

¼ cup (60 ml) extra-virgin olive oil, plus more for drizzling

Smoked paprika, for finishing

1 tablespoon chopped parsley leaves, for finishing

This is one of my favorite ways to make use of hot embers: nestling eggplant in the coals until it's blistered and blackened to the point of looking burnt. Once you slice it open, you'll be surprised to find tender, smoky flesh that is easily made into baba ghanoush. Slather it over toasts or Grilled Sesame Flatbread (page 70), or serve it as a fire-kissed dip with crunchy veggies.

Prepare a wood fire or coals for cooking (see page 22) and allow the flames to die out until you have a nice bed of hot embers.

Place the eggplant directly onto the hot embers. Grill, turning occasionally, until the eggplant has collapsed, the flesh is soft, and the skin is charred, 15 to 20 minutes. Transfer to a cutting board and let cool.

Cut the eggplant in half lengthwise. Scoop out the flesh and transfer to a large bowl. Using a fork, mash the eggplant to a chunky consistency. Add the tahini, garlic, lemon juice, and salt and continue to mash together. Drizzle in the olive oil, continuing to mash to combine. Season with more salt, if needed. Transfer to a serving bowl, drizzle with more olive oil, and sprinkle with paprika and the parsley to finish. Serve warm or cold.

Store leftovers in an airtight container in the refrigerator for up to 3 days.

EMBER-ROASTED LEEKS WITH **RICOTTA** AND ANCHOVY-WALNUT CRUNCH

SERVES 4

4 large leeks, tough green tops and roots trimmed off

⅓ cup (40 g) toasted chopped walnuts

3 oil-packed anchovy fillets

2 garlic cloves

2 strips of lemon peel

½ teaspoon kosher salt, plus more to taste

2 lemon wedges

Freshly ground black pepper

½ cup (125 g) fresh ricotta

Extra-virgin olive oil, for drizzling

Leeks have a high sugar content, which makes them ideal for caramelization and charring. Cooking them over coals until they're blackened on the outside allows the interior to steam until they reach a melt-in-your-mouth texture. Top them off with extra umami from an anchovy-walnut crunch and dollops of creamy ricotta for contrast. Serve the leeks as an ideal side dish to a sizzling Cowboy Steak with Gochujang Chile Butter (page 122).

Soak the leeks in a bowl of cold water for 10 minutes, gently squeezing to remove any dirt. Pat dry.

To make the anchovy-walnut crunch, place the walnuts, anchovies, garlic, lemon peels, and salt on a cutting board. Using a knife, chop the ingredients together to form a coarse paste. Transfer to a small bowl and set aside.

Prepare a wood fire or coals for cooking (see page 22) and allow the flames to die out completely, until you have a nice bed of hot embers.

Place the leeks directly onto the hot embers. Rotate the leeks occasionally and cook until they are deeply charred on the outside and feel soft in the centers, 15 to 20 minutes. Once they are ready, transfer them to a board and slice in half lengthwise through the root ends. Peel away the charred outer layer and transfer cut side up to a serving plate. Squeeze the lemon wedges over the leeks and season with salt and pepper. Top with dollops of the ricotta, the anchovy-walnut crunch, and a drizzle of olive oil, and serve.

SWEET POTATOES WITH CHILE BUTTER

SERVES 4

4 medium sweet potatoes
(such as Japanese or purple
sweet potatoes)

Gochujang Chile Butter
(page 226)

Flaky sea salt

Spiced Furikake (page 95) or
store-bought furikake, for
sprinkling

SPECIAL EQUIPMENT

Heavy-duty aluminum foil

Sweet potatoes were practically made to be buried under hot coals; once they emerge, their natural sweetness comes forward and they become meltingly tender. Split open the skins and top the creamy flesh with a pat of umami-rich Gochujang Chile Butter and a sprinkle of furikake for texture.

Prepare a wood fire or coals for cooking (see page 22) and allow the flames to die out until you have a nice bed of hot embers.

Wrap each sweet potato tightly in foil and press to seal. Nestle the potatoes onto the hot coals, scooping the remaining embers over and around the sweet potatoes to bury them. Let them roast, rotating occasionally, until the potatoes are tender throughout, 40 minutes to 1 hour. Set aside to cool for a few minutes, brushing away any ashes.

Split the potatoes open and top each with a dollop of chile butter. Season with flaky salt and a sprinkle of furikake to finish.

STUFFED BANANA BOATS

SERVES 4

4 bananas

One 1.5-ounce (42 g) chocolate bar, broken into pieces

1 cup (55 g) mini marshmallows

2 cinnamon graham crackers, crumbled

SPECIAL EQUIPMENT

Heavy-duty aluminum foil

If you've never treated yourself to a banana boat, you're in for a delicious surprise. It's a mashup of a s'more and a banana split, making it the ideal dessert as the night winds down by the fire. Here's how it's done: split a banana in its peel in half, load it up with your favorite toppings, wrap it snugly in foil, and cozy it up to the hot coals to cook. Start off with the classic trio of chocolate chunks, marshmallows, and crumbled graham crackers, or let your imagination run wild with other tasty combos.

Prepare a wood fire or coals for cooking (see page 22) and allow the flames to die out until you have a nice bed of hot embers.

Cut a banana vertically down the center, not all the way through, just enough for the knife to graze the peel on the bottom. Spread the banana slightly apart. Stuff chocolate pieces into the banana. Wrap the banana in foil to seal.

Place the banana boat onto the embers. Cook until the banana is soft and the chocolate has melted, flipping halfway through, about 10 minutes total. Carefully unwrap the banana and stuff with marshmallows. Wrap the banana back up in the foil to warm through until the marshmallows are melty. Sprinkle with crumbled graham crackers to finish and eat while warm.

VARIATIONS

Tropical
Chocolate + raspberries + chopped mango + marshmallows + coconut flakes

Strawberry Hazelnut
Nutella + strawberries + marshmallows + chopped hazelnuts

PB&J
Peanut butter + chocolate + berry jam + marshmallows + crushed peanuts

Salted Caramel
Chocolate + caramel sauce + marshmallows + flaky sea salt

CAMPFIRE COOKING

Cooking while camping is one of the highlights of any outdoor adventure. There's something truly special about preparing food over an open flame, making the cooking process a memorable part of the experience. Whether you're whipping up a hearty skillet breakfast, making pudgy pies for lunch, or cooking a cozy Dutch oven dinner, the campfire becomes a central gathering spot, turning mealtime into a shared moment. The ambience is also unique—cooking under the stars, surrounded by nature's sounds, and enjoying a meal in the fresh air are incredibly fulfilling.

To make campfire cooking easier and more enjoyable, it's key to prep as much as possible before you head out. A little preparation at home can go a long way at the campsite. For instance, to lighten your packing load, take only the exact amounts of ingredients you need. Wash, peel, and trim veggies ahead of time to minimize waste and make for easier cleanup. Chop any veggies that can be prepped in advance without losing quality. Also, prepare your sauces, dressings, and marinades at home and store them in airtight containers in your cooler. If you plan on baking or making Dutch oven dishes with baked toppings, mix your dry ingredients beforehand.

For a super-easy mealtime solution, consider foil packet meals. You can prep and fill the foil packets at home, then store them in your cooler until you're ready to cook. Alternatively, invest in a few pie irons and just pack your sandwich ingredients for a quick and tasty meal. And if you're looking for more ideas, check out the Recipes Good for Camping list on page 233. With a bit of planning, campfire cooking can become an unforgettable part of your outdoor adventure.

The rustic charm of Dutch oven cooking is perfectly suited to the open fire. Many of us have Dutch ovens in our kitchens, but taking it outdoors is a whole different experience. It's important to note that you should use a *camp Dutch oven*, which has little feet that allow it to hover over hot coals and a special flanged lid where you can add more hot coals if you're using it for roasting or baking.

One of the exciting features of the camp Dutch oven is creating two-in-one combo meals, like Vegetarian Chili Topped with Cornbread, which takes advantage of the Dutch oven's ability to make stews and bake at the same time. Or go for the iconic Rustic Beef Bourguignon with meltingly tender beef. And for dessert, it's high drama with a flambéed Bananas Foster Upside-Down Cake.

There are different kinds of coals you can use for Dutch oven cooking (read more on page 22). For some recipes, coal briquettes are suggested as the best way to standardize the heat for cooking. That doesn't mean you can't create your own coals from firewood or use lump charcoal. Using briquettes is just a way to maintain steady, even heat that works extremely well for baking or any dishes that are cooked low and slow.

When it comes to temperature control with hot coal briquettes, an easy guideline is to use twice as many briquettes as the diameter of your Dutch oven in inches (for cooking at 350°F/180°C). So a 10-inch (25 cm) Dutch oven would call for around 20 briquettes. Place about one-third of the briquettes underneath in a ring and distribute the rest evenly on top. Have a few extra on hand in case you want to crank up the heat.

VEGETARIAN CHILI TOPPED WITH CORNBREAD

SERVES 4

FOR THE CORNBREAD TOPPING

¾ cup (120 g) fine-ground cornmeal

¾ cup (95 g) all-purpose flour

¼ cup (55 g) packed light brown sugar

1 teaspoon baking powder

½ teaspoon baking soda

½ teaspoon kosher salt

1 cup (240 ml) whole milk

6 tablespoons (85 g) unsalted butter, melted and slightly cooled, plus pats of butter for serving

1 large egg, lightly beaten

2 tablespoons honey, plus more for serving

FOR THE CHILI

2 tablespoons extra-virgin olive oil

1 yellow onion, diced

4 garlic cloves, finely grated

2 teaspoons chili powder

1 teaspoon ground cumin

2 tablespoons tomato paste

Ingredients continue

Using a Dutch oven offers the perk of cooking hearty vegetarian chili and fluffy cornbread together, creating a satisfying one-pot meal. As we know from dishes like shepherd's pie, there's just something cozy about layering comfort foods that is the ultimate upgrade. Scoop out heaping spoonfuls and enjoy around the fire.

Prepare 23 hot coal briquettes (plus 2 or 3 extra) for cooking (see page 22). First, place a chimney in the middle of your firepit. Then, fill it with charcoal briquettes. Next, toss some crumpled newspaper or a couple of fire starters in the chamber underneath. Ignite the paper or fire starters. As the coals heat up, you'll notice them turning gray and ash-covered. They should be ready in 15 to 20 minutes.

Make the cornbread: Put the cornmeal, flour, brown sugar, baking powder, baking soda, and salt in a large bowl and stir to combine. Stir the milk, butter, egg, and honey into the dry ingredients until just combined. Set aside.

Carefully pour the coals from the chimney into your firepit. Arrange 7 of the coals in a ring to provide a base for the Dutch oven, distributing them evenly. Keep the remaining hot coals on one side of the firepit so they are easy to access.

Make the chili: Place the Dutch oven over the ring of hot coals. Pour in the olive oil and heat until shimmering. If you need to increase the heat, add a few more coals underneath. Add the onions, garlic, chili powder, and cumin and cook, stirring occasionally, until the onions are soft and translucent, 5 to 7 minutes. Add the tomato paste, chipotle chile, and adobo sauce and cook until the color deepens,

1 chipotle chile in adobo, chopped, plus 1 teaspoon adobo sauce

One 15-ounce (425 g) can black beans, drained and rinsed

One 15-ounce (425 g) can kidney beans, drained and rinsed

One 14.5-ounce (411 g) can diced fire-roasted tomatoes

2 teaspoons kosher salt

1 cup (240 ml) chicken or vegetable broth

FOR SERVING

Grated Cheddar, diced onions, and sour cream

SPECIAL EQUIPMENT

10-inch (25 cm/4-quart) cast-iron camp Dutch oven

another 1 to 2 minutes. Add the beans, tomatoes, salt, and broth, stirring to combine.

Pour the cornbread batter over the chili, smoothing into an even layer. Cover the Dutch oven with its lid and evenly distribute 16 hot coals on top.

Bake for 25 to 35 minutes, until the cornbread is cooked through and a toothpick inserted in the center comes out clean. Set aside to cool for 10 minutes.

Scoop out the chili and cornbread to serve. Have guests finish their chili with grated Cheddar, diced onions, and sour cream, and smear the cornbread with butter and honey.

Store leftovers in an airtight container in the refrigerator for up to 4 days.

GOLDEN CHICKEN AND DUMPLINGS

SERVES 6

FOR THE DUMPLINGS

1½ cups (190 g) all-purpose flour

1½ teaspoons baking powder

¼ teaspoon baking soda

1½ teaspoons sugar

¾ teaspoon kosher salt

1 cup plus 2 tablespoons (265 ml) buttermilk

2 tablespoons unsalted butter, melted

FOR THE CHICKEN STEW

2 tablespoons extra-virgin olive oil

2 pounds (910 g) boneless, skinless chicken thighs, cut into 1-inch (2.5 cm) pieces

½ teaspoon kosher salt, plus more to taste

Freshly ground black pepper

4 tablespoons (55 g) unsalted butter

1 medium yellow onion, diced

2 celery stalks, chopped

3 medium carrots, peeled and cut into ¼-inch (64 mm) rounds

3 garlic cloves, smashed

2-inch (5 cm) piece ginger, peeled and grated

Ingredients continue

Turmeric and ginger add an earthy, spiced kick and vivid golden hue to classic chicken and dumplings. Tender chunks of chicken thighs are simmered in a hearty stew packed with veggies and topped with cloudlike fluffy dumplings. The dumpling batter is dropped right onto the stew, before the pan is covered and topped with hot coals to finish baking.

Prepare 24 hot coal briquettes (plus 2 or 3 extra) for cooking (see page 22). First, place a chimney in the middle of your firepit. Then, fill it with charcoal briquettes. Next, toss some crumpled newspaper or a couple of fire starters in the chamber underneath. Ignite the paper or fire starters. As the coals heat up, you'll notice them turning gray and ash-covered. They should be ready in 15 to 20 minutes.

Make the dumplings: Place the flour, baking powder, baking soda, sugar, and salt in a large bowl and stir until combined. Slowly stir the buttermilk and melted butter into the dry ingredients until just combined. Set aside.

Carefully pour the coals from the chimney into your firepit. Arrange 8 of the coals in a ring to provide a base for the Dutch oven, distributing them evenly. Keep the remaining hot coals on one side of the firepit so they are easy to access.

Make the chicken stew: Place the Dutch oven over the ring of hot coals. Pour in the olive oil and heat until shimmering. If you need to increase the heat, add a few more hot coals underneath. Add the chicken and season with the salt and a few grinds of pepper. Cook the chicken, stirring occasionally, until it turns opaque (it doesn't need to be completely cooked through), 3 to 4 minutes. Transfer the chicken to a bowl, leaving any bits in the pot, and set aside.

Recipe continues

¼ cup (30 g) all-purpose flour

2 teaspoons ground turmeric

5 cups (1.2 L) chicken stock

⅓ cup (80 ml) heavy cream

¼ cup (15 g) chopped
fresh dill

SPECIAL EQUIPMENT

12-inch (30 cm/6-quart)
cast-iron camp Dutch oven

Add the butter to the pot and let it melt. Add the onions, celery, carrots, garlic, and ginger. Stir to scrape up any browned bits from the bottom. Cook until the vegetables soften, 3 to 5 minutes. Stir in the flour and turmeric, stirring constantly for 1 to 2 minutes. Season with salt and pepper.

Return the chicken to the pot and stir in the stock. Cook, stirring occasionally, until the chicken is cooked through and the liquid has thickened, about 5 minutes. Stir in the heavy cream. Season with salt and pepper.

Using a spoon, drop generous dollops of the dumpling dough onto the stew, leaving some space in between to puff up as they cook.

Place the lid on the Dutch oven and evenly distribute the remaining 16 coals on top, aiming for a temperature of about 350°F (177°C). Bake, undisturbed, for 20 to 25 minutes, until the dumplings are completely cooked through (pale but puffy).

Remove the lid and divide the chicken and dumplings among bowls, sprinkling with the dill to serve.

Store leftovers in an airtight container in the refrigerator for up to 3 days.

BEER-STEAMED MUSSELS WITH CHORIZO

SERVES 4

4 ounces (115 g) Spanish chorizo sausage or soppressata, casing removed, cubed

2 tablespoons extra-virgin olive oil, plus more for brushing

1 large shallot, chopped

2 garlic cloves, thinly sliced, plus 1 whole clove

½ teaspoon red pepper flakes

Kosher salt and freshly ground black pepper

10 ounces (280 g) cherry tomatoes, halved

1 cup (240 ml) light beer (such as pale ale or lager)

4 pounds (1.8 kg) fresh mussels, cleaned

4 thick slices country bread

Flaky sea salt

2 tablespoons chopped parsley leaves

SPECIAL EQUIPMENT

12-inch (30 cm/6-quart) cast-iron camp Dutch oven

A big ol' pot of mussels is an impressive and surprisingly easy dish to cook for a group. The shells open once they're finished cooking, revealing tender, briny bites. Ladle these into bowls for your guests and remember to spoon up some of the tasty broth and chorizo that collects at the bottom of the pot.

Prepare a fire for medium heat (see page 20) and set a grate over it. Make sure your grate is secured to hold the Dutch oven.

Place the Dutch oven on the grate. Put the chorizo in the pot and cook until browned and crispy, 3 to 4 minutes. Add the olive oil to the pot. Once the oil is shimmering, add the shallots, sliced garlic, and red pepper flakes. Season with kosher salt and black pepper. Cook until the shallots soften, 4 to 5 minutes.

Stir in the tomatoes and beer and simmer for about 30 seconds, until the alcohol burns off. Stir in the mussels. Cover with the lid and cook until the mussels have opened, 5 to 8 minutes. Discard any mussels that have remained closed.

Meanwhile, brush the bread slices with olive oil and grill them until char marks appear, 2 to 3 minutes. Remove from the heat. Rub the clove of garlic against the crisped edges. Cut the toasts into halves and sprinkle with flaky salt.

Sprinkle the parsley over the mussels and serve with the toasts alongside for dipping.

RUSTIC BEEF BOURGUIGNON

SERVES 6

6 slices thick-cut bacon, cut into ½-inch (1.3 cm) pieces

2 pounds (910 g) boneless beef chuck roast, cut into 1½-inch (3.75 cm) cubes

½ teaspoon kosher salt, plus more to taste

Freshly ground black pepper

8 ounces (225 g) baby bella mushrooms, quartered

3 medium carrots, peeled and cut into ½-inch (1.3 cm) rounds

10 ounces (280 g) shallots, peeled and cut into halves (quartered if large)

1 medium yellow onion, chopped

3 garlic cloves, finely grated

2 tablespoons tomato paste

¼ cup (30 g) all-purpose flour

3 cups (720 ml) beef stock

2 cups (480 ml) full-bodied red wine (such as zinfandel or cabernet)

3 thyme sprigs, plus thyme leaves for garnish

1 bay leaf

Crusty baguette slices, for serving

SPECIAL EQUIPMENT

12-inch (30 cm/6-quart) cast-iron camp Dutch oven

This classic hearty beef stew is ideal for a leisurely cookout. When planning for a longer simmer, make sure to have extra hot coals on standby. You'll need to replenish your hot coals to keep the Dutch oven on a low simmer; this low and slow cooking allows those deep flavors to meld together and ensures tender, melt-in-your-mouth chunks of beef.

Prepare 24 hot coal briquettes (plus 2 or 3 extra) for cooking (see page 22). First, place a chimney in the middle of your firepit. Then, fill it with charcoal briquettes. Next, toss some crumpled newspaper or a couple of fire starters in the chamber underneath. Ignite the paper or fire starters. As the coals heat up, you'll notice them turning gray and ash-covered. They should be ready in 15 to 20 minutes.

Carefully pour the coals from the chimney into your firepit. Arrange 8 of the coals in a ring to provide a base for the Dutch oven, distributing them evenly. Keep the remaining hot coals on one side of the firepit so they are easy to access.

Place the Dutch oven over the ring of hot coals. Put the bacon in the pot and cook for 8 to 10 minutes, until crisp and browned. If you need to increase the heat, add a few more hot coals underneath. Transfer the bacon to a large bowl and set aside, leaving the fat in the pot.

Add the beef to the pot and season with salt and pepper. Cook, stirring occasionally, until the beef is browned on all sides, 5 to 7 minutes. Transfer the beef to the bowl with the bacon.

In the remaining bacon fat, add the mushrooms and cook until golden, 2 to 3 minutes. Transfer the mushrooms to another bowl. Add the carrots and shallots and cook until softened, about 5 minutes. Season with salt and pepper.

Transfer the chunky veggies to the same bowl as the mushrooms and set aside.

Add the onions to the pot, stirring and cooking until soft, 5 to 7 minutes. Add the garlic and tomato paste and cook for 2 minutes. Add the flour and cook for another 2 minutes. Stir in the stock and wine, stirring constantly to dissolve the flour. Add the beef, bacon, thyme, bay leaf, the ½ teaspoon salt, and a few grinds of pepper, stirring to combine.

Place the lid on the Dutch oven and evenly distribute the remaining 16 hot coals on top, aiming for a temperature of about 350°F (177°C). Cook undisturbed for 1 hour.

Begin to prepare another batch of 17 hot coals about 15 minutes before your hour mark, using the same process as before, to replenish the ones that have cooled down. If you find yourself running out of room in your pit to light your chimney, try placing it on the grate of another grill or on fire-safe bricks placed on the ground.

Remove the cooled coals from the lid. Stir in the cooked veggies. Replace the lid and place the new hot coals on top. Cook for another 30 minutes, or until the beef is falling apart and fork-tender. Remove the pot from the heat. Season the stew with salt and pepper as needed. Sprinkle with thyme leaves and serve with baguette slices on the side.

Store leftovers in an airtight container in the refrigerator for up to 3 days.

PEACH AND BLUEBERRY COBBLER

SERVES 6 TO 8

Ingredients continue

FOR THE FRUIT FILLING

2 pounds (910 g) ripe peaches or 6 cups thawed frozen peaches, sliced

1 cup (6 ounces/170 g) blueberries

½ cup (100 g) plus 2 tablespoons granulated sugar

2 tablespoons cornstarch

1 tablespoon fresh lemon juice

1 teaspoon vanilla extract

½ teaspoon ground cinnamon

½ teaspoon ground ginger

Kosher salt

FOR THE BISCUIT TOPPING

1 cup (125 g) all-purpose flour

⅓ cup (80 g) fine-ground cornmeal

¼ cup (50 g) granulated sugar

2 teaspoons baking powder

½ teaspoon kosher salt

8 tablespoons (115 g) unsalted butter, cold, cut into cubes, plus more for greasing

⅔ cup (160 ml) buttermilk, plus more for brushing

Coarse sugar, for sprinkling

Vanilla ice cream, for serving

The flavor of ripe peaches shines in this cobbler, a quintessential summertime dessert. A biscuit-like topping sits over a warm, sweet fruit filling—and of course, topping it off with scoops of ice cream is a must. If you don't have fresh, seasonal peaches or blueberries, frozen is your next best option. The peaches should be thawed first; the blueberries can be frozen until ready to mix and bake.

Make the filling: In a large bowl, combine the peaches, blueberries, granulated sugar, cornstarch, lemon juice, vanilla, cinnamon, ginger, and a pinch of salt, stirring gently. Cover and set aside in a cool spot.

Make the biscuit topping: In another bowl, whisk together the flour, cornmeal, granulated sugar, baking powder, and salt. Add the butter cubes and use a fork to cut them into the flour mixture until pea-size pieces form. Stir in the buttermilk until just combined. Cover loosely and set aside.

Prepare 23 hot coal briquettes for cooking (see page 22). First, place a chimney in the middle of your firepit. Then, fill it with charcoal briquettes. Next, toss some crumpled newspaper or a couple of fire starters in the chamber underneath. Ignite the paper or fire starters. As the coals heat up, you'll notice them turning gray and ash-covered. They should be ready in 15 to 20 minutes.

Carefully pour the coals from the chimney into your firepit. Arrange 7 of the coals in a ring to provide a base for the Dutch oven, distributing them evenly. Keep the remaining hot coals on one side of the firepit so they are easy to access.

Grease the inside of the Dutch oven with butter to prevent sticking. Spoon the fruit filling into the Dutch oven, along with any juices. Drop large spoonfuls of biscuit topping all

SPECIAL EQUIPMENT

10-inch (25 cm/4-quart)
cast-iron camp Dutch oven

over, leaving some space in between. Brush the topping with buttermilk and sprinkle with coarse sugar. Place the lid on the Dutch oven.

Place the Dutch oven over the ring of hot coals and evenly distribute 16 hot coals on top, aiming for a temperature of about 375°F (191°C). Bake, undisturbed, for 35 to 45 minutes, until the cobbler topping is browned and a toothpick inserted in the topping comes out with only a few moist crumbs attached. Let cool for 10 minutes before serving. Scoop the warm cobbler warm into bowls and serve with ice cream.

BANANAS FOSTER UPSIDE-DOWN CAKE

FOR THE TOPPING

6 tablespoons (85 g) unsalted butter, melted

¾ cup (165 g) packed dark brown sugar

4 firm bananas, peeled and cut lengthwise into halves

FOR THE CAKE

1½ cups (190 g) all-purpose flour

1½ teaspoons baking powder

1 teaspoon ground cinnamon

½ teaspoon kosher salt

¼ teaspoon baking soda

6 tablespoons (85 g) unsalted butter, at room temperature

½ cup (110 g) packed dark brown sugar

¾ cup (150 g) granulated sugar

2 large eggs, at room temperature

1 cup (225 g) mashed ripe bananas (about 2 bananas)

½ cup (120 ml) buttermilk

1 teaspoon vanilla extract

1 cup (120 g) chopped walnuts

¼ cup (60 ml) dark rum (80 to 100 proof), optional

Vanilla ice cream, for serving

SPECIAL EQUIPMENT

10-inch (25 cm/4-quart) cast-iron camp Dutch oven

Heavy-duty aluminum foil

Get ready for a showstopping dessert: flambéed bananas Foster cake. This decadent treat combines the classic flavors of bananas Foster with a moist, banana bread–like cake studded with walnuts. But here's where the magic happens: for the grand finale, you'll flambé the banana topping with a splash of rum. With each bite, you'll taste the sweet caramelized bananas, hints of cinnamon, and a subtle kick from the rum.

Line the Dutch oven with foil on the bottom and sides.

Make the topping: Pour the melted butter into the Dutch oven, coating the bottom. Using a pastry brush, spread the butter to grease the sides of the pot. Sprinkle the bottom with the brown sugar and smooth with the back of a spoon to evenly coat. Arrange the banana slices in a single layer, cut side down over the mixture, trimming to fit if needed.

Make the cake: In a bowl, stir together the flour, baking powder, cinnamon, salt, and baking soda. Set aside.

In a large bowl, using an electric mixer, cream the butter until smooth. Add the brown sugar and granulated sugar gradually and beat until fluffy, about 3 minutes. Add the eggs, one at a time, beating well after each addition. Mix in the mashed bananas. Add half of the dry ingredients, mixing until well incorporated. Add the buttermilk, vanilla, and the remaining dry ingredients and mix well. Fold in the walnuts to combine. Spoon the batter into the prepared Dutch oven with a spatula and smooth the top evenly. Cover with the lid.

Prepare 20 hot coal briquettes for cooking (see page 22). First, place a chimney in the middle of your firepit. Then, fill it with charcoal briquettes. Next, toss some crumpled newspaper or a couple of fire starters in the chamber underneath. Ignite the paper or fire starters. As the coals heat up, you'll notice them turning gray and ash-covered. They should be ready in 15 to 20 minutes.

Carefully pour the coals from the chimney into your firepit. Arrange 7 of the coals in a ring to provide a base for the Dutch oven, distributing them evenly. Keep the remaining hot coals on one side of the firepit so they are easy to access.

Place the Dutch oven over the ring of hot coals. Evenly distribute 13 hot coals on top, aiming for a temperature of about 350°F (177°C).

Bake for 35 to 45 minutes, until the cake is browned and cooked through and a toothpick inserted in the center comes out clean. Remove from the heat and let the cake rest for 15 minutes. Carefully turn the cake onto a serving platter.

If using the rum, heat it in a small saucepan over the hot coals for 1 to 2 minutes (do not let it boil). Remove the pan from the heat. Using a long-reach lighter, carefully ignite the rum and pour it over the top of the cake. Once the flames die out, serve the cake warm with scoops of vanilla ice cream.

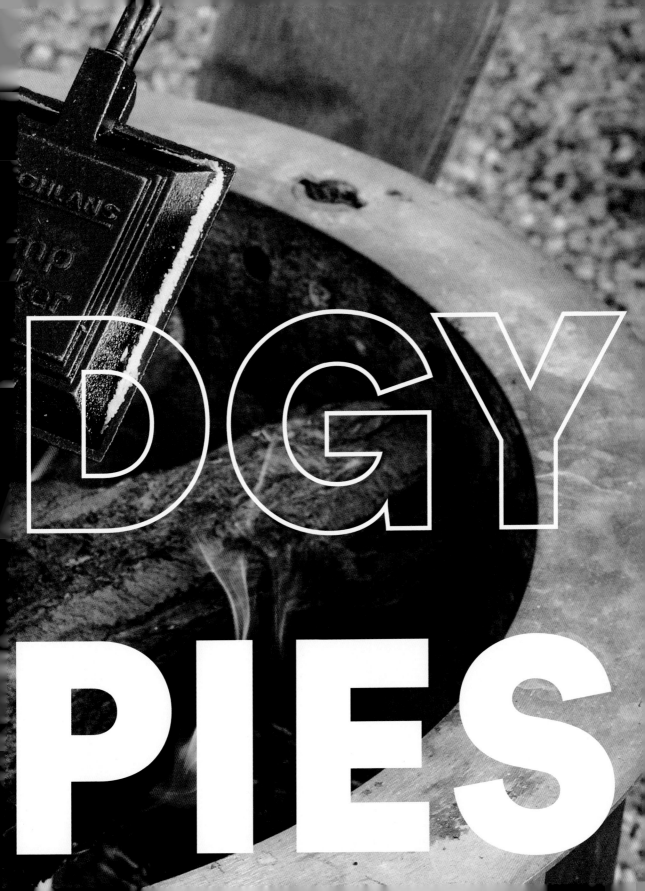

DGY
PIES

The pudgy pie iron is a low-key cooking tool easy to find at outdoor-gear shops. There is something adorably retro Americana about it. This simple device, consisting of two cast-iron chambers hinged together that can be hovered over a campfire, is used to make sandwiches and sweet and savory pies.

I've crafted dozens of incredible pudgy pies, sharing my love for them with everyone who's had a taste. Some of the classics like grilled cheese sandwiches and apple hand pies always please; more adventurous options include the Croque Monsieur Pudgy Pie and Spanakopita Pudgy Pie. For those of you with a sweet tooth, if you're a chocolate banana lover, don't miss the S'mores Choconana Pudgy Pie, topped with toasted gooey marshmallows.

Simple sliced sandwich bread works best for pudgy pies; the size fits just right in the pie iron, ensuring that all your fillings will seal perfectly. This meal comes together quickly since you can cook over flames—no need to wait for the fire to die down. Using a pie iron with long handles gives you control over the heat while hovering your sandwich over the fire.

Once you get the hang of it, invest in a few pie irons and host pudgy pie night. Let your friends and family build their own with an assortment of fillings, both sweet and savory—and best of all, they get to cook for themselves.

FANCY PIZZA POCKETS

MAKES 1

1 tablespoon unsalted butter, melted

2 slices sourdough or white Pullman bread, about ½ inch (1.3 cm) thick

2 tablespoons Basic Tomato Sauce (page 222) or store-bought tomato sauce

¼ cup (30 g) shredded low-moisture mozzarella

1 tablespoon grated Parmesan

4 slices pepperoni

4 slices soppressata

Pinch of red pepper flakes

SPECIAL EQUIPMENT

Pie iron

Remember Hot Pockets, every kid's after-school favorite? Well, this version is all grown up and even more delicious. It's got that same irresistible, cheesy pizza goodness packed inside but is kicked up a notch with soppressata, pepperoni, and a blend of cheeses.

Prepare a fire for cooking (see page 17). Allow the fire to simmer down, so the logs are mostly red-hot embers rather than roaring flames.

Generously brush the insides of the pie iron with the melted butter. Place one slice of the bread into the bottom half of the iron. Spread with 1 tablespoon of the tomato sauce and sprinkle with the mozzarella and Parmesan, leaving a ½-inch (1.3 cm) gap around the edges. Add the pepperoni and soppressata. Sprinkle with the red pepper flakes. Spread the remaining 1 tablespoon tomato sauce over the other slice of bread and place spread side down on top of the sandwich. Close the pie iron and clamp shut. Using a knife, trim any overhanging crusts off the bread.

Begin by hovering or propping the pie iron in a spot that is away from the flames but still quite hot, 6 to 10 inches (15 to 25 cm) from the embers, adjusting as needed. Turn the iron occasionally, until the bread is a deep golden brown (carefully open and check after a few minutes) and the cheese is melted, 7 to 10 minutes. If the sandwich sticks to the pie iron, use a knife to skim the edges and help loosen the sandwich. Cut into halves and serve warm.

CROQUE MONSIEUR PUDGY PIE

MAKES 1

1 tablespoon unsalted butter, melted

2 slices sourdough or white Pullman bread, about ½ inch (1.3 cm) thick

4 teaspoons mascarpone cheese

¼ cup (25 g) shredded Gruyère

2 slices smoked ham

1 slice Swiss cheese

Grainy mustard, for spreading

SPECIAL EQUIPMENT

Pie iron

If you're a fan of classic croque monsieur sandwiches, this pudgy pie version will send you over the edge. Cooking this sandwich in a pie iron results in a wonderfully crisp, golden exterior that is stuffed with creamy mascarpone, gooey cheese, and smoky ham. Serve it with a few cornichons or your favorite pickles on the side. To make an extra-decadent croque madame, top it with a fried egg.

Prepare a fire for cooking (see page 17). Allow the fire to simmer down, so the logs are mostly red-hot embers rather than roaring flames.

Generously brush the insides of the pie iron with the melted butter. Place one slice of the bread into the bottom half of the iron. Spread with 2 teaspoons of the mascarpone and sprinkle with the Gruyère, leaving a ½-inch (1.3 cm) gap around the edges. Fold and add the ham slices and top with the Swiss cheese. Spread the mustard and the remaining 2 teaspoons mascarpone over the other slice of bread and place spread side down on top of the sandwich. Close the pie iron and clamp shut. Using a knife, trim any overhanging crusts off the bread.

Begin by hovering or propping the pie iron in a spot that is away from the flames but still quite hot, 6 to 10 inches (15 to 25 cm) from the embers, adjusting as needed. Turn occasionally, until the bread is a deep golden brown (carefully open and check after a few minutes) and the cheese is melted, 7 to 10 minutes. If the sandwich sticks to the pie iron, use a knife to skim the edges and help loosen the sandwich. Cut into halves and serve warm.

CUBAN PUDGY PIE

MAKES 1

1 tablespoon unsalted butter, melted

2 slices sourdough or white Pullman bread, about ½ inch (1.3 cm) thick

Mayonnaise, for spreading

1 slice smoked ham

4 slices salami

4 slices pickle chips

2 slices Swiss cheese

Yellow mustard, for spreading

SPECIAL EQUIPMENT

Pie iron

Here's a twist on the classic Cuban sandwich: instead of slow-cooked pork, you'll use a convenient combo of sliced deli smoked ham and salami. Bring all your ingredients outside on a sheet pan for easy assembly. Layer your sandwich ingredients onto one side of your iron. Don't worry if your pile starts looking high; once you clamp the iron closed, it'll seal in every tasty bite.

Prepare a fire for cooking (see page 17). Allow the fire to simmer down, so the logs are mostly red-hot embers rather than roaring flames.

Generously brush the insides of the pie iron with the melted butter. Place one slice of the bread into the bottom half of the iron. Spread with mayonnaise. Fold and add the ham and salami slices and top with the pickles and Swiss cheese, leaving a ½-inch (1.3 cm) gap around the edges. Spread mustard over the other slice of bread and place spread side down on top of the sandwich. Close the pie iron and clamp shut. Using a knife, trim any overhanging crusts off the bread.

Begin by hovering or propping the pie iron in a spot that is away from the flames but still quite hot, 6 to 10 inches (15 to 25 cm) from the embers, adjusting as needed. Turn occasionally, until the bread is a deep golden brown (carefully open and check after a few minutes) and the cheese is melted, 7 to 10 minutes. If the sandwich sticks to the pie iron, use a knife to skim the edges and help loosen the sandwich. Cut into halves and serve warm.

FIGGY PIGGY
PUDGY PIE

MAKES 1

1 tablespoon unsalted butter, melted

2 slices sourdough or white Pullman bread, about ½ inch (1.3 cm) thick

1 tablespoon store-bought fig jam

2 slices provolone

2 tablespoons crumbled blue cheese

2 thin slices prosciutto

SPECIAL EQUIPMENT

Pie iron

Balancing the perfect blend of sweet and savory, this figgy piggy sandwich bursts with bold flavors. Imagine this: luscious fig jam mingling with smoky slices of prosciutto, all topped with gooey provolone and bold blue cheese, each bringing its distinctive flavor to this decadent sandwich.

Prepare a fire for cooking (see page 17). Allow the fire to simmer down, so the logs are mostly red-hot embers rather than roaring flames.

Generously brush the insides of the pie iron with the melted butter. Place one slice of the bread into the bottom half of the iron. Spread with the fig jam, add the provolone slices, sprinkle with the blue cheese, and top with the prosciutto slices, leaving a ½-inch (1.3 cm) gap around the edges. Finish with the remaining bread slice. Close the pie iron and clamp shut. Using a knife, trim any overhanging crusts off the bread.

Begin by hovering or propping the pie iron in a spot that is away from the flames but still quite hot, 6 to 10 inches (15 to 25 cm) from the embers, adjusting as needed. Turn occasionally, until the bread is a deep golden brown (carefully open and check after a few minutes) and the cheese is melted, 7 to 10 minutes. If the sandwich sticks to the pie iron, use a knife to skim the edges and help loosen the sandwich. Cut into halves and serve warm.

SPANAKOPITA PUDGY PIE

MAKES 1

⅓ cup (50 g) thawed and drained frozen chopped spinach

¼ cup (40 g) crumbled feta cheese

1 large egg

1 garlic clove, finely grated

1 tablespoon chopped fresh dill

Kosher salt and freshly ground black pepper

Pinch of ground nutmeg

3 tablespoons unsalted butter, melted

One 13-by-18-inch (33 by 46 cm) sheet filo pastry

SPECIAL EQUIPMENT

Pie iron

Picture flaky, delicate layers of filo baking up crispy, with a cheesy spinach filling for a pudgy twist on spanakopita. Any excess filo that overhangs gets folded into the pie iron so not a single bite is wasted. The pie makes a perfect appetizer for two when sliced in half, but I suggest making a few more while you're at it—they're just too delicious not to make extra.

In a bowl, combine the spinach, feta, egg, garlic, and dill. Season with a big pinch of salt, a few grinds of pepper, and the nutmeg. Set aside.

Prepare a fire for cooking (see page 17). Allow the fire to simmer down, so the logs are mostly red-hot embers rather than roaring flames.

Generously brush the insides of a pie iron with some of the melted butter. Place one corner of the sheet of filo pastry into the bottom half of the iron, leaving any overhang. Brush butter over the corner section. Fold the filo in half crosswise, brush with butter, then fold in half vertically (to form 4 layers), brushing with butter to finish. Fill with the spinach and feta mixture. Fold the overhanging filo pastry over the filling to seal. Close the pie iron and clamp shut.

Begin by hovering or propping the pie iron in a spot that is away from the flames but still quite hot, 6 to 10 inches (15 to 25 cm) from the embers, adjusting as needed. Turn occasionally, until the filo is crispy and golden brown (carefully open and check after a few minutes) and the cheese is melted, 7 to 10 minutes. If the pastry sticks to the pie iron, use a knife to skim the edges and help loosen. Cut into halves and serve warm.

S'MORES CHOCONANA PUDGY PIE

MAKES 1

1 tablespoon unsalted butter, melted

2 slices sourdough or white Pullman bread, about ½ inch (1.3 cm) thick

Tahini, stirred smooth, for spreading

1 ounce (30 g) bittersweet chocolate bar, broken into pieces

½ banana, peeled and sliced crosswise

Pinch of flaky sea salt

2 marshmallows

SPECIAL EQUIPMENT

Pie iron

Long metal roasting skewers, or wooden sticks cleaned and soaked in water for at least 30 minutes

Here's a grown-up s'more made with dark chocolate, bananas, and a hint of creamy tahini for earthy balance. While your pudgy pie is cooling down, toast a few marshmallows to add extra gooey decadence on top.

Prepare a fire for cooking (see page 17). Allow the fire to simmer down, so the logs are mostly red-hot embers rather than roaring flames.

Generously brush the insides of the pie iron with the melted butter. Place one slice of the bread into the bottom half of the iron. Spread with tahini and top with the chocolate, banana slices, and salt, leaving a ½-inch (1.3 cm) gap around the edges. Finish with the remaining bread slice. Close the pie iron and clamp shut. Using a knife, trim any overhanging crusts off the bread.

Begin by hovering or propping the pie iron in a spot that is away from the flames but still quite hot, 6 to 10 inches (15 to 25 cm) from the embers, adjusting as needed. Turn occasionally, until the bread is a deep golden brown (carefully open and check after a few minutes) and the chocolate is melted, 7 to 10 minutes. If the sandwich sticks to the pie iron, use a knife to skim the edges and help loosen the sandwich. Transfer the sandwich to a plate to cool slightly.

Toast the marshmallows on skewers over the fire. Top the sandwich with marshmallows to finish. Cut into halves and serve warm.

SALTED HONEY APPLE PUDGY PIE

MAKES 1

¼ small tart-crunchy apple (such as Pink Lady or Honeycrisp), cored, thinly sliced

1 teaspoon fresh lemon juice

1 teaspoon sugar

½ teaspoon ground cinnamon

1 tablespoon unsalted butter, melted

2 slices sourdough or white Pullman bread, about ½ inch (1.3 cm) thick

Honey, for spreading

Flaky sea salt

Ice cream, for topping (optional)

SPECIAL EQUIPMENT

Pie iron

Low effort, high reward—this dish is reminiscent of an old-fashioned apple hand pie, except it doesn't take hours to make. Salted honey-glazed apples make up the filling that gets nestled in a golden crust. The key? Slice the apples super thin, so they cook through just right. To take the pie up a notch, serve it à la mode.

Prepare a fire for cooking (see page 17). Allow the fire to simmer down, so the logs are mostly red-hot embers rather than roaring flames.

In a bowl, toss the apple slices with the lemon juice, sugar, and cinnamon to coat.

Generously brush the insides of the pie iron with the melted butter. Place one slice of the bread into the bottom half of the iron. Spread with honey and layer the apple slices, leaving a ½-inch (1.3 cm) gap around the edges. Spread honey over the other slice of bread, sprinkle with flaky salt, and place spread side down on top of the sandwich. Close the pie iron and clamp shut. Using a knife, trim any overhanging crusts off the bread.

Begin by hovering or propping the pie iron in a spot that is away from the flames but still quite hot, 6 to 10 inches (15 to 25 cm) from the embers, adjusting as needed. Turn occasionally, until the bread is a deep golden brown (carefully open and check after a few minutes), 7 to 10 minutes. If the sandwich sticks to the pie iron, use a knife to skim the edges and help loosen the sandwich.

Cut into halves and serve warm topped with ice cream, if desired.

PEACH AND RASPBERRY PUDGY PIE

MAKES 1

½ ripe peach, pitted, thinly sliced

¼ cup (30 g) raspberries

2 teaspoons fresh lemon juice

2 teaspoons sugar

½ teaspoon ground cinnamon

1 tablespoon unsalted butter, melted

2 slices sourdough or white Pullman bread, about ½ inch (1.3 cm) thick

Ice cream or whipped cream, for topping (optional)

SPECIAL EQUIPMENT

Pie iron

The flavors in this pie are an ode to summer, but don't let chilly weather keep you from making it; thawed frozen fruit works well, too. The buttery crust is filled with juicy peaches and tart raspberries, with lemon juice to balance out the sweetness of the fruit. Finish it off with a scoop of ice cream or a dollop of freshly whipped cream.

Prepare a fire for cooking (see page 17). Allow the fire to simmer down, so the logs are mostly red-hot embers rather than roaring flames.

In a bowl, toss the peach slices and raspberries with the lemon juice, sugar, and cinnamon to coat.

Generously brush the insides of the pie iron with the melted butter. Place one slice of the bread into the bottom half of the iron. Fill with the peach-raspberry mixture, leaving a ½-inch (1.3 cm) gap around the edges. Finish with the remaining bread slice. Close the pie iron and clamp shut. Using a knife, trim any overhanging crusts off the bread.

Begin by hovering or propping the pie iron in a spot that is away from the flames but still quite hot, 6 to 10 inches (15 to 25 cm) from the embers, adjusting as needed. Turn occasionally, until the bread is a deep golden brown (carefully open and check after a few minutes), 7 to 10 minutes. If the sandwich sticks to the pie iron, use a knife to skim the edges and help loosen the sandwich.

Cut into halves and serve while warm topped with ice cream or whipped cream, if desired.

EVERY

E

GO-WITH-THING BASICS

To boost a dish from pretty good to jaw-droppingly incredible, use sauces, dressings, and even flavored butters. These accompaniments create balance and elevate your food to the next level. Just think about your average grilled veggies with olive oil and S+P. Now imagine the same veggies slathered in a spiced Gochujang Chile Butter. Yeah, you can thank me later.

This group of essentials includes my favorite go-with-everything basics. While many recipes in this book already include sauces and dressings, the ones with the most versatility are gathered here. From zesty sauces to flavorful compound butters, each can add a punch of personality to your dishes. Whether you're whipping up a casual weeknight dinner or hosting a backyard barbecue for friends, these go-with-everything basics will become your backbone for delicious outdoor cooking.

GARLICKY AIOLI

HERBY FETA

GOCHUJANG BUTTER

WALNUT ROMESCO

LEMONY YOGURT SAUCE

**MAKES ABOUT 1 CUP
(240 G)**

1 cup (240 g) plain Greek
yogurt

Zest of 1 lemon and juice
of ½ lemon

1 garlic clove, finely grated

Kosher salt

This simple yogurt sauce complements grilled vegetables
and smoky meats wonderfully; the tanginess from lemons
adds brightness to nearly any dish. Feel free to adjust the
consistency by adding a splash of water if you prefer a runnier
sauce for drizzling. Use it on Cumin Grilled Carrots (page 37)
or as a dipping sauce for Lamb Kofta Kebabs (page 141).

Combine the yogurt, lemon zest, lemon juice, and garlic in
a small bowl. Season with salt to taste. Serve immediately
or store in an airtight container in the refrigerator for up
to 3 days.

WHIPPED HERBY FETA

**MAKES ABOUT 1¼ CUPS
(285 G)**

One 8-ounce (225 g) block
feta cheese, crumbled

¼ cup (60 g) plain whole-milk
Greek yogurt, plus more as
needed

Zest of 1 lemon and
2 teaspoons lemon juice

1 garlic clove, smashed

2 tablespoons chopped fresh
herbs (preferably mint, basil,
or dill)

1 tablespoon extra-virgin
olive oil

Freshly ground black pepper

This versatile creamy dip can be scaled up easily if you're
feeding more than a few. It's perfect as a dip for crudités or
as a spread for grilled toasts. The fresh herbs and lemon add
a bright, zingy lift to the creamy feta and yogurt. Feel free to
switch up the herbs with any tender herbs you have on hand.

In a food processor or blender, combine the feta, yogurt,
lemon zest, lemon juice, garlic, herbs, and olive oil. Blend or
process until smooth, scraping down the sides as needed.
If the mixture needs thinning, add more yogurt by the
tablespoon until it reaches the desired consistency. Season
with pepper. Serve immediately or store in an airtight
container in the refrigerator for up to 2 days. Whipped feta
will continue to thicken in the refrigerator.

NOTE: *If you're camping or don't have a food processor or
blender at home, mash the feta in a small bowl with a fork,
then mix in the rest of the ingredients. You'll end up with
a chunkier texture, but it will be just as delicious.*

BASIC TOMATO SAUCE

**MAKES ABOUT 2½ CUPS
(570 G)**

One 28-ounce (794 g) can
whole peeled San Marzano
tomatoes

¼ cup (60 ml) extra-virgin
olive oil

1 medium yellow onion,
chopped

3 garlic cloves, thinly sliced

Red pepper flakes

Kosher salt

½ cup (20 g) torn basil leaves

Consider this your go-to versatile tomato sauce for spreading
over pizza, dunking Garlic Bread Twists (page 131)—and
dressing pasta, of course. Made with canned tomatoes, garlic,
and fresh basil, it's an easy 30-minute sauce.

In a medium saucepan, combine the tomatoes (with their
juices), olive oil, onions, garlic, and a pinch of red pepper
flakes. Season with a generous pinch of salt. Bring the
sauce to a simmer over medium-high heat, then reduce
the heat so the sauce cooks at a slow, steady simmer for
30 minutes. Stir occasionally and use a wooden spoon to
crush the tomatoes as they cook and soften.

Remove the saucepan from the heat, add the basil, and
blend until smooth with an immersion blender. Alternatively,
transfer the sauce to a blender to blend (with caution if the
sauce is hot). Season with salt. The sauce keeps covered
in the refrigerator for up to 4 days, or frozen for up to
6 months.

EASY GARLICKY AIOLI

**MAKES ABOUT 1 CUP
(220 G)**

⅓ cup (80 ml) neutral oil (such as canola or avocado oil)

1 large egg

1 large egg yolk

2 garlic cloves, finely grated

1 tablespoon fresh lemon juice

½ teaspoon kosher salt, plus more to taste

⅓ cup (80 ml) extra-virgin olive oil

Traditional aioli is made with time and patience as garlic and olive oil emulsify slowly in a mortar and pestle. This is a cheater's version that comes together in under 5 minutes with the help of an immersion blender (I promise this is real aioli—not just flavored mayo). Despite the temptation to add the olive oil at the beginning of the process, the key is to transfer the aioli to a bowl halfway through and finish whisking in the olive oil by hand. Skipping this step might result in a bitter aioli. This luscious sauce comes together quickly and easily; it's the ideal accompaniment for potatoes, grilled meats, and seafood.

Place the neutral oil, egg and egg yolk, garlic, lemon juice, and salt in a 1-quart (950 ml) mason jar. Place an immersion blender all the way to the bottom of the jar and switch it on. As the aioli begins to thicken, tilt and lift the immersion blender until the mixture is emulsified.

Transfer the aioli to a bowl. Using a whisk, slowly stream in the olive oil, blending to thicken it to a creamy consistency. Taste and adjust the salt as needed. Serve immediately, or store in the jar, sealed, in the refrigerator for up to 2 days. The aioli will continue to get thicker and more garlicky the longer it sits.

NOTE: *If you don't have an immersion blender, you can use a food processor for the first step. Make sure to transfer the aioli to a bowl to finish whisking by hand or else it will become bitter.*

ANY GREENS PESTO

**MAKES ABOUT 1 CUP
(250 G)**

½ cup (60 g) nuts of choice
(toasted walnuts, almonds,
pecans, or pistachios), or
pumpkin seeds

¼ cup (25 g) grated Parmesan

2 garlic cloves, smashed

2 cups (80 g) greens of choice
(such as chopped basil,
parsley, cilantro, arugula,
kale, radish tops, beet greens,
or spinach)

Juice of ½ lemon

¼ cup (60 ml) extra-virgin
olive oil

½ teaspoon kosher salt

Freshly ground black pepper

You can keep it loose and easy when it comes to what goes in
your pesto. Use the same basic formula and incorporate what's
available in your fridge—parsley, radish tops, kale, and arugula
can all make tasty alternatives, and feel free to mix them up.
It's the addition of toasted nuts (and yes, it's okay to substitute
for the traditional pine nuts, too), salty cheese, and olive oil
that make pesto so delicious.

Place the nuts, Parmesan, and garlic in a food processor
and pulse until finely ground. Add your greens and the
lemon juice and pulse again. With the motor still running,
slowly stream in the olive oil until the pesto is smooth, about
1 minute. Add the salt and season with pepper to taste. The
pesto can be made a day ahead and stored in an airtight
container in the refrigerator.

NOTE: *If you have a Bullet blender, you can toss everything
in and blend; just use a spoon or small spatula to scrape
down the sides from time to time to make sure it is well
combined.*

CHARRED SCALLION BUTTER

MAKES ABOUT ½ CUP (115 G)

Neutral oil (such as canola or avocado oil), for brushing

4 scallions, roots trimmed off

1 teaspoon extra-virgin olive oil

¾ teaspoon kosher salt, plus more to taste

Freshly ground black pepper

8 tablespoons (115 g) unsalted butter, at room temperature

Zest of 1 lemon and 1 tablespoon lemon juice

This is the ultimate goes-with-everything compound butter. Charred, smoky scallions are folded into a bright, citrus-infused butter. Try spreading it over Grilled Sesame Flatbread (page 70) or melting it onto sizzling steaks. To make this compound butter, you'll only need a few scallions.
Pro tip: toss the whole bunch onto the grill, keep some scallions for this recipe, and save the rest for a tasty side addition to meats and seafood.

Prepare a fire for medium-high heat (see page 20), set a grate over it, and brush the grate with oil.

Place the scallions on a sheet pan and drizzle with the olive oil to coat. Season with salt and pepper.

Set the scallions on the grill and cook, turning once, until blackened grill marks appear and the white bulbs are tender, 4 to 5 minutes total. Transfer to a cutting board to cool, then coarsely chop.

Using a fork, mash the scallions with the butter, lemon zest, lemon juice, the ¾ teaspoon salt, and a few grinds of pepper until evenly combined. The compound butter can be made up to 1 week ahead and stored in an airtight container in the refrigerator.

GOCHUJANG CHILE BUTTER

MAKES ABOUT ½ CUP (115 G)

8 tablespoons (115 g) unsalted butter, at room temperature

1½ tablespoons gochujang

1 garlic clove, finely grated

¾ teaspoon kosher salt

Umami-rich, spicy, and funky—gochujang upgrades your butter, giving it a flavorful punch. The spread is something you'll want to keep in your rotation for smearing over steaks, grilled corn, and sweet potatoes.

Place the butter, gochujang, garlic, and salt in a small bowl. Mash together with a fork until evenly combined. The butter can be made up to 1 week ahead and stored in an airtight container in the refrigerator.

SWEET 'N' JAMMY CARAMELIZED ONIONS

MAKES ABOUT ½ CUP (120 G)

2 tablespoons unsalted butter

2 large yellow onions, peeled, halved, and thinly sliced

Kosher salt

Sweet and jammy onions are a breeze to make, but they do demand a bit of time and patience to allow the onions to reach caramelized mahogany-hued perfection. Use them as a condiment for outdoor cookouts nestled into burgers (page 113), as a topping on pizza (page 102), or served alongside grilled meats. When you're planning for a cookout, make these onions on your kitchen stovetop ahead of time. Set aside about an hour and be sure to hang around to give them a stir every now and then.

Melt the butter in a large skillet over medium heat. Add the onions and stir to coat in the butter. Spread the onions out evenly over the pan, giving them more space and allowing them to caramelize. Season with a generous pinch of salt.

Reduce the heat to medium-low and continue to cook, stirring occasionally to prevent the onions from sticking. After another 15 minutes, the onions should begin to turn golden brown. Add a splash of water if the onions begin to burn, and scrape up any bits stuck to the bottom of the pan. Continue cooking and stirring until the onions become dark brown and take on a jammy consistency, 45 minutes to 1 hour total.

Season to taste with salt. Let cool, then transfer to an airtight container and refrigerate for up to 1 week.

ACKNOWLEDGMENTS

Judy Pray, thank you for having the vision to bring this project to life. Your generous support and guidance gave me the courage to share my voice with others. And to the Artisan team, it's been an honor working with you. I learned to cook from your books and am grateful for the opportunity to inspire a new generation of cooks.

Chris Morocco and Sarah Jampel, the team at *Bon Appétit*, thanks for spotting my camping adventures and featuring me in your summer outdoor cooking issue (dream come true!)—a moment that ultimately led to the creation of this cookbook. Gratitude to everyone who worked on the story with me: Zaynab Issa, Bettina Makalintal, Rachel Lasserre, Peden+Munk, Hannah Ferrara, and Malcolm Smitley.

To my literary agent, Andrianna deLone at CAA, thank you for answering my many questions, giving me guidance, and helping to shape this book.

Dylan Gordon, thank you for beautifully capturing the natural beauty of California and the joy of sharing meals with friends.

My Ojai food ladies—Casey Dobbins, Rebecca Taylor, and Chase Elder—I'm grateful for the opportunity to collaborate with all of you on this book. Your artistic touch in the kitchen made these dishes beautiful.

To my sponsors: Year & Day, Heller, and The Get Out, thanks for making the food in this book look delicious with your tabletop pieces.

My family: Debbie Yen, who did it all—from assisting me on the shoot to taste-testing most of the dishes in this book; Donna Yen, my lifelong hype woman and sous-chef; and my dad, Lyoni Yen, who dragged us to almost every national park as kids and shared his passion for the great outdoors.

I couldn't have done it without your support. Thank you and I love you.

A special thanks to some of the best cooks and food writers I know—Andy Baraghani, Elizabeth Poett, Kerry Diamond, and Camille Becerra—for supporting this book with your seal of approval. Your work has been a constant source of inspiration to me over the years.

My dear friends, I love you all so much. Thank you for supporting me and being the best eaters I know: Quy Nguyen, Avril Nolan, Erika Chou, Lars Beaulieu, Jade Lai, the McClain sisters, Sean Dooley, Philip and Sarah Andelman, Marc and the Armitano family, Cathy Hahn, David Burden, Britt Cox, Daniel Moldow, Camilla Engstrom, Cameron Richards, Phoebe Sung and Peter Buer, Nathan Williams, Nick Nemecheck, Niels Christophersen, Jesse Huber, Ish Goldstein, April Lee, and Portia Wells.

RESOURCES

FIREPITS

Breeo
breeo.com
Stylish and durable smokeless firepits that make a statement in your backyard while also providing a quality cooking experience. They have a large capacity, meaning you don't need to worry about feeding the fire as often, and they take both wood and charcoal.

Solo Stove
solostove.com
Sleek stainless-steel smokeless firepits that can be outfitted with a whole line of fun accessories to cook with. They come in portable sizes that make it easy to take the stove anywhere. It is recommended to use wood with these firepits.

Barebones
barebonesliving.com
This rustic, classic cowboy-style firepit is ideal for a pared-down cooking experience. It has a large, wide bowl that you can use with both wood and charcoal. Barebones also carries a wide range of cooking tools and tabletop products ideal for outdoor entertaining.

WOOD, CHARCOAL, AND FIRE STARTERS

Cutting Edge Firewood
cuttingedgefirewood.com
High-quality firewood that comes precut if using an ax ain't your thing.

Cowboy Lump Charcoal
cowboycharcoal.com
Quality lump charcoal that's easy to light, keeps lasting heat, and creates a wonderfully smoky flavor.

Kingsford Charcoal Briquettes
kingsford.com
Most of the time if I'm using briquettes, I'm cooking in a Dutch oven and looking for steady, even heat. The Professional line of charcoal burns the hottest, or you can use Kingsford's Low and Slow briquettes if you're aiming for a longer cooking time.

Fatwood
fatwood.com
The best all-natural wood fire starters.

Fire and Flavor Biomass Fire Starters
fireandflavor.com
All natural, eco-friendly fire starters.

COOKWARE, TOOLS, AND ACCESSORIES

CAST-IRON PANS
Lodge
lodgecastiron.com

Field Company
fieldcompany.com

CAMP COOKING SETUPS
Snow Peak
snowpeak.com

COOLERS
Yeti
yeti.com

PIE IRONS
Coghlans
coghlans.com

GRILLING TONGS
Traeger
traeger.com

FIRE-SAFE GLOVES
Grill Armor Gloves
grillarmorgloves.com

RAPIDFIRE CHIMNEY STARTER
Weber
weber.com

INSTANT-READ THERMOMETER
Thermapen
thermoworks.com

BASTING BRUSH
OXO
oxo.com

GRILL BRUSH
Grillart
grillartus.com

RECIPES GOOD FOR CAMPING

INDEX

Note: Page numbers in *italics* indicate photos of recipes.

DIANA YEN is a cookbook writer, photographer, and food stylist living in Ojai, California. She is the author of *A Simple Feast*. Her projects with leading food and lifestyle brands focus on the simplicity and elegance of everyday meals. With a background in home and lifestyle design, she strives to bring a sense of beauty and community to the table. Yen's recipes, photography, and writing have been featured in *Kinfolk, Cherry Bombe, Bon Appétit, Saveur, Food & Wine, Epicurious,* and many other publications. Follow her on Instagram at @diana_yen_.